Scientific Integration of Queries on Inner Human Life

Dr. H. Prashad

Books For All

Delhi-110052

First Published 2013

ISBN 13: 978-81-7386-296-0
ISBN 10: 81-7386-296-6

Published By
BOOKS FOR ALL
(an imprint of Low Price Publications)
A-6, Second Floor, Nimri Commercial Centre,
Ashok Vihar Phase-4, Delhi - 110 052
Tel.: +91 11 2730 2453
website: www.Lppindia.com
e-mail: info@Lppindia.com

Printed At
IIP Printers, D-17, Raja Garden, New Delhi
Phone: 25441120

PRINTED IN INDIA

Dedicated To

The Almighty, Cosmic Power, Supernal and Silence Formless Oneness, whose Blessings, Radiance, Continued Inspiration, Booming Energy and Silent Guidance that has graced me to follow the path of Peace and Enlightenment for realizing the Ultimate Truth and Self – Realization and to be always being in Him for ultimate mergence in the Absolute.

December 2012 **Dr. Har Prashad**

With Deep Devotion and Humble Gratitude

The thoughts, in general, behind various queries given in this book are from the light source of evolved soul, the direct disciple of Param Guru Sri Sri Mahaavatar Babaji, besides humble contribution that of the author.

The evolved soul is endeavoring to extricate SRI VIDYA, the king of Vidyas, from the morass it had been discarded to, and restore it to its pristine glory.

Expression of my humble gratitude to the evolved soul is a very meager gesture bestowed to him in comparison to the wisdom and source light he had transmitted and planted in me. The outcome of this book is just a direct glimpse of his grace and blessings.

Dr. Har Prashad

Benediction

Being "Spiritual" is to be close to the spirit, to the Self, to the Soul/Atma and finally to be merged with the Supernal, and being in that glorious light. If one merges in the Supernal or comes in its magnetic field, he gradually becomes magnetized with time and there remains no difference between him and Him. He speaks, acts and thinks through Him. His life, its purpose and aims all belong to the Supernal and he lives for Him only. This is the state of being in self and this is the Self-realization.

Dr. Har Prashad came in my contact a decade back. He was sufficiently spiritually ripe before he met me. I found him true seeker of the truth. He was very fearless and asked me such queries that at time I was amazed of his spiritual enlistment. I could understand that his queries cannot be dealt unless one has self experienced and had Anu bhities. His association with me got strengthened close spiritual ties and at time I invited his queries to address my disciples. A few spiritual highly mysterious queries, I declined to discuss so as not to disclose to public. However, he found the solution in himself by the grace of Cosmic Mother and Blessings of Mahaavatar Babaji.

His complete life revolved around spirituality from his early age. Being all-alone, after losing his parents in 1947, he was emigrated from West Pakistan during partition. He was brought up entirely under the grace of Almighty and could rise and become internationally renowned Scientist/Engineer in his field of Tribology and got Doctorate in this field. As I understand, even being in horizontal life his mental travel was skyward by following the pathless path of spirituality so as to achieve the highest by his efforts and by grace of the cosmic power.

His thought of writing this book was by the will and command of the God. To deal with highly mysterious subject without the grace of Cosmic Mother is not possible. It is self-less service of the author towards humanity, spirituality and to the cosmic power by whose grace this book was accomplished. In spite of completely involved with technical work, and family responsibilities, he could devote time for the divine accomplishment, which is itself a mysterious divine grace on him. I consider Dr. Prashad as a blessed soul. He has been bestowed this grace by the divine Mother for the enlistment of spirituality in the spiritual aspirants/Sadhakas, and for the posterity.

I wish the readers of this book to get self-evolved in the spirituality like the author himself so that their mysterious queries get solutions/answers by the grace of Cosmic Power. I also wish the author and readers all the success in their cause less cause of self-evolution and realization.

May Cosmic Power, Cosmic Mother and Mahaavtar Babaji bless all of us to ascend in the pathless path of spirituality?

Param Para Vishwambhara **"Ananda ghana"**

Dr. Ariparala Vishwam

Preface

I do not know how, when and why the "Self – realization" became the sole aim of my life since my early age. I left no stone unturned within my resources and capabilities to know more and more about the spiritual sciences to fulfill the causeless cause of my life. I have gone through the Self-realization lessons by Sri Sri Pramahansa Yogananda Ji and took Diksha/initiation for Kriya yoga in my early age and practiced for decades.

In due course, I experienced transformation in my personality, thoughts and deeds. The evolution, taking place inwardly was vividly crystal clear but the queries of the mind related to spiritual matters were so mysterious that I could not get solutions to satisfy myself. However, my inner silence, by God's grace always guided me to probe more and more of this mystery. The available literature for mysterious experiences/Anubhuties being very sketchy and distorted has created immense confusion and ambiguity in my mind till I met The "Evolved Soul". I could trap mysterious source wisdom by God's grace and Blessings, and particularly could focus on serious mysterious queries, which I was trying to probe for confirmation and re-confirmation. By self experience and by deep Anubhuties/realization of a source light of an evolved soul I could ascertained the type of mysterious experiences, I had undergone. I could visualize in the "Evolved Soul" a direct divine source light of Sri Sri Mahaavatar Babaji.

By the grace of Absolute – Absolute, seeds have been procreated in my thoughts to express the rare experiences I was bestowed by His grace for the sincere seekers for the truth. This made me to write the book on "Scientific Integration of Queries on Inner Human Life". This book is written in 18 chapters in the forms of mysterious queries and is based on the wisdom as if transmitted by Almighty like Yama to Nichiketa.

The queries, their explanations and logics are all mysterious and may be beyond the understanding of fresh seeker of the truth but feel of the mysterious spiritual wisdom by self experiences / Anubhuties shall be the asset in due course. This book will be precious priceless treasure for the sincere and real seekers of the truth following the scientific path of Self-realization for mergence with the Supernal in this life and for all those who wanted to be being in the light source and become light in true sense by the grace of Paramatma / Almighty / and Absolute – Absolute.

Finally, the purpose of this book is to enlighten those spiritual aspirants, who are in doubt despite having made a considerable progress in the path of self – realization. I present these queries with solutions in all humility by the Blessings of Almighty and Sri Sri Mahaavtar Babaji with the hope that it will enlighten them to follow this pathless path of mergence of their soul with Supernal in this life.

Once again, my sincere and humble gratitude to the Formless One-ness, which inspired me to take up this unique work of its kind for the true seekers of the Absolute – Absolute. I would also like to express my gratitude to my wife – Darshan, my loving son-Poojan, daughter-in-law Gauri, my beloved daughter-Shwetlana and son-in-law, Rajeev & little Kriya and loving Nimay who have silently co-operated with me to accomplish this divine assignment for the true seekers of truth.

December 2012 **Dr. Har Prashad**

12533, South Surrey,

28th Avenue,

V4a 2n8

Canada

Mobile: 91-9652013280 (India)

Mobile: 1-604-825-5139 (Canada)

Email: har.prashad@gmail.com

About the Author

Dr. Har Prashad is presently advisor for Tribology of Rtec, USA. He is retired Senior Deputy General Manager (Tribology) from the Bharat Heavy Electricals Limited, Corporate Research and Development Division, Hyderabad (India) in 2004. He was consultant of Centre for Tribology Inc (CETR), USA till August 2011. He obtained an M.E. (Hons) degree in Mechanical Engineering in 1970, and subsequently, Ph.D. in Tribology. He worked with the Indian Institute of Petroleum, Dehra Dun, and with the Design Bureau at Bokaro Steel Ltd., Dahnbad, Bihar, before joining BHEL in 1974.

Dr. Prashad has published more than 125 papers in both national and international journals, reviewed more than 200 technical papers and many Ph.D. thesis. He is the author of seven technical books. The book on "Tribology in Electrical Environments" is published from United Kingdom by Elsevier Publishers in December 2005. The second book on 'Solving Tribology Problems of Rotating Machines "is published by Wood head Publishers, U.K, in February 2006. The third book on "Integral Approaches to Tribo-testing in Mechanical Engineering" is published by CRC, USA in August 2009. Four books are published by Lap publishing, Germany in 2011: Behaviour of Rolling-element Bearings under Shaft Voltages; Electrical Analogy of Different types of Journal & Thrust Bearings; A System Approach to Mechanical Engineering Problems; and "Anti-friction Bearings and Lubricants under Electrical Currents".

For his achievements, author's name has been included in Marquis Who's Who in the world published in 2001 and 2012 from USA. Also, his name was included in International Directory of Distinguished Leadership-2001, published by American

Biographical Institute. His bio-data is published in the directory of "Contemporary Who's who 2004" and in 2012 by the same institute. Also, "Scientific Award of Excellence 2011" has been awarded by the same Institute. Furthermore, for his distinguished achievements Tribology Society of India graced him with Life Time Achievement Award 2010 (Industrial Category) in the Seventh International Conference on Industrial Tribology-2010, held at Ranchi (Organized by Sail Authority of India under the Aegis of Tribology Society of India) on 4th December 2010.

Besides the above technical books, the book of spiritual sciences on "Solutions of Problems & Remedies of Human Life—A Path of Peace and Enlightenment" is published in August 2010 by lpp, DK's Books for All, New Delhi. The same publisher has published the book on "Japu Ji Sahib and Srimad Bhagavad-Gita – The Spark of Enlightenment" in 2011. The book on "Spikes of Deep Silence by Silence and in Silence" has been published in 2012. Furthermore the e-book on "Know Thyself" has been published by Yellow publishers of U.K. in 2011. . A book on "Dormant Human Science" is published by Lap Lambert Academic Publishing, Germany in January 2012. Also, books on "Mysterious Life Waves", "Unison at Core", "Retrieving the Immersed Subjective Science" "Multifaceted Approach of being Conscious and Creative—The Integral vision" and "Life is Continuum with Discontinuities-Glimpses of Self in Self" have been published by Lap. Besides being author of these books, he is pursuing the evolved work on the book on "Extension of Life through Manifestation of Consciousness— to be Beyond Time & Space with Discontinuities".

Contents

Chapter 1

A God Realized Soul

1.1 How does a seeker of the absolute truth, a spiritual aspirant/Sadhaka, knows that he has finally found a God Realized, the most appropriate Guru, he was searching for?

Now a day to find a God Realized, the most appropriate Guru for the neophyte Sadhaka, a true seeker of absolute truth, is an uphill and the most difficult task. Without the grace of Almighty, it is not possible to come across such a realized personality. There are number of show-masters and Mayavik Gurus who are fully involved in worldly activities, are all around us. There are chances that initial seeker after truth, in search of a real master, may get trapped in the clutches of such false cheaters and get cheated and lose his faith in masters and in divinity. But, he must remain determined and genuine to the spiritual cause. The days will not be far away when the great Cosmic Mother and her omnipresent force and blessings may assist him if the real seeker after truth continues his efforts to find the real spiritual path. This may happen even if he has only a limited exposure/understanding of spirituality and knowledge of the divine path. Within no time he will find that he is with the appropriate personalities, he is looking for. He being a true seeker cannot get stuck with the false Gurus if he is genuine and determined in his spiritual practices. In the Gita Lord Krishna states (Ch 4:11) "As all surrender unto me I reward them accordingly". Positively his intrinsic true magnetic desires will take him to an appropriate correct source. The Cosmic Mother by her own unknown mysterious channels will take him to such a source, a more relevant path, without much of his searching effort, which may enhance his search after the absolute truth. Under the guidance of truly divine personality, gradually, he will find that the spiritual evolution in him is much faster and soon he will discover that he is in the hands of a Sat Guru/true master.

Initially, he may not visualize, but gradually as peace and silence in him increases, he will witness the magnetism of the Sri Guru/master that makes him understand that he is with the right personality, and he is looking for. He will be mentally guided without his knowledge. And soon he will find that where he was stuck, those barriers have disappeared. The flow of divine energy, which may have been blocked or impeded, now continues to surge in him without any disruption. This will give him more and more satisfaction, peace and happiness. By the grace of the Sri Guru, he is in close contact with; all his mental barriers will be washed away and within no time his heart discovers that he got all that he ever wanted. In case the Sadhaka is quite advance in spiritual Sadhana, he may able to recognize some key divine symptoms in the Sri Guru. Some of these are:

Radiance and glow in the face of the Guru; his stillness of eyeballs; and also automatic movement of the life force in the spinal cord of the Sadhaka merely by the presence of the guru; are the clear indication of true master. With these unmistakable signs, the Sadhaka will leave no-doubt about the superiority of the Sat Guru as compared to the other gurus. The Sadhaka conforms within himself that he has come to the appropriate Guru; he was looking for and searching. On the contrary, a common materialistic man with merely horizontal desires may or may not be able to assess whether they are with the real Sat Guru or not since they look for the material gains and nothing else. They don't know the pathless path of the travel in the vertical spiritual plane. For such people spiritual science has no meaning. Such people just come to the master and go. For them just blessing of the Guru is sufficient for the material gain. True magnificence of the Guru is hidden from them until such times till they become qualified for the guru's guidance to take the vertical path of spiritual evolution.

Chapter 2

Life Force, Divine Light and Supreme Romance

2.1 What is life force? How does and when life force becomes the divine light?

Before understanding the concept of life force, one needs to understand clearly the basic concept of Prana. Prana is a subtle force. Prana is the life of a jeeva. Life force or Prana is the subtle energy, which animates the gross body. If Prana leaves/goes out of the body, the body cannot survive, body collapses (e.g. at death). Therefore Prana is the basis for survival. One can sustain his body without solid food and water for some time depending on the reserves of body, but without Prana (in gross words breath), it is a merely a question of a few moments only.

Prana is a part of the breath that goes/travels automatically to different physical organs during all the states of the body. Prana is a subtle energy contained within the breath that goes in and out by itself. The breath is God and as we cannot live without the mercy of God and so we cannot survive without breath. The breath, which we take, gets converted in different constituents as soon as it enters the body. Breath has all the constituents required for sustaining the body/life since we breath in void/Akasha, which contains in subtle form all the five basic elements i.e. earth/solid, water, fire/ agni, air/Prana, Akasha/ether. That is why some yogis can sustain themselves for years together by knowing the art of perfect breathing and converting the various constituents of the breath in different constituents as required by the body and its various systems.

Prana is a part of the air, we breathe. Part of the inhaled air gets converted into Prana as it enters in our lungs through the nostrils. This undifferentiated Prana is further get transformed/changed into different type i.e.Vyana Prana, Samana Prana, and Apana Prana. These transformations occur from the main Prana in the human system as this Prana passes through heart center / Dhahara chakra and other energy charkas downwards in the body. How all these transformation takes place, is still the mystery to be solved and understood. Presently, this whole process of bio-mechanism of all these transformations is beyond imagination.

Vyana Prana after getting transformed from the main undifferentiated Prana/breathe, performs the activities of circulation and governs the circulation of vital force and energy through out the entire body systems. In other words, Vyana Prana governs the circulation of subtle Pranic energy in 72000 nerves of the entire system. If the transformation of Pranic energy to Vyanic Pranic energy is not appropriate and robust, then the some parts of the body is deprived of the Pranic energy and different physical problems start originating from those parts of the body where this Pranic energy has not able to reach. Then various existing dormant physical problems are likely to manifest in the body. Acupuncture therapy, to some extend, is helpful in diverting this energy to such locations where acupuncture is made, provided there has been the transformation to Vyana Pranic energy from Pranic energy, and there is only resistance in the passage of flow of energy of Vyana Prana. Basically Vyana Prana acts as the medium for transportation of various Pranic energies.

Part of the main/undifferentiated Pranic energy is transformed and converted into the Samana Prana/energy. This energy is required for the proper functioning of all the vital systems of the body. Basically Vyana Prana transports and distributes the Samana energy/Prana depending on the need of the particular vital system of the body. Therefore, every main system and auxiliary body system get Pranic energy by the required proportion by Samana Prana through the Vyana Prana.

Another important function of the body is its excretory system; by this system toxins and excreta of the body are removed. The

Apana Prana governs this activity of the body, which is another constituent of the main/undifferentiated Pranic energy. The removal of all types of body toxins is totally governed by the Apana energy/ Prana. Any disturbance in the Apana energy system, its conversion from the main Pranic energy and distribution etc. can lead to all the related problems of the system. Medicines taken for rectification of the vital system for overcoming varieties of such problems help temporarily. Under the effect of medicines with less of Pranic energy, the system starts functioning for a short interval but effects of medicines can eventually deteriorate the system and lead to the permanent damage. Basically, in absence of any of the Pranic energies including Apana, Vyana, Samana and Prana, assistance of medicines/tonics for rectification is very temporary, and the system reverts back to the non-functional mode as soon as the catalytic effect of the medicines is over. In short, Prana and Pranic energy is the God given divine nectar/ Amrit, that helps us to live healthy, and happily without the use of external medicines. The body has the capability to rectify the various systems by the help of different Pranic energies.

Apart from the Pranic energies of different types, as discussed above, there is a very important pranic energy known as Udana Prana, which is the main source of life force. This Udana Prana is the main source of life and is itself the divine energy required for the self-realization. This needs to be generated in the system by yogic practices under the direction of Sat Guru/true master and by the blessings of God's grace. This divine energy of Udana Prana ultimately awakens the Kundalini, and by its vertical travel through the spinal cord, it gets transformed into the divine light and acts as the carrier of soul to the Supernal. This is the highest secret in the path of self-realization. This, if achieved, will be the highest achievement of the human life in his birth. This leads to Savikalpa to Nirvikalpa Samadhi and final mergence with the Supernal. But, all this is feasible by the grace of Almighty; Guru kripa/blessings; and even to start this activity by the self-efforts is possible by His grace only.

The Udana Prana can be generated in the system by the help of the most sacred and secret techniques given by Guru Ji and

Mahaavatar BabaJi. Nowhere in spiritual literature, have these types of techniques been discussed. Only the aim of human life and the art of living etc. have been described in sufficient details. Basically, the very close interaction of Apana Prana with Vyana Prana along with Samana Prana releases the magnetically charged spiritual atoms in the Udana in the Nabhi/navel centre of the human system. The interaction of these Pranas to create Udana prana is the essence of the Kriya Yoga techniques. The magnetically charged spiritual energy atoms, thus released by the interaction of various Pranas, get aligned by the presence of the existing Pranic energies, and generate a flow of Pranic electronic force in the Udana, in the navel area. This aligned flow of charged electrons- -"Lifetrons" is named as Udana Prana.

The Udana Prana can also be generated by repetition /japa of sacred Mantras by concentrating on the navel centre and deeply listening the same mentally as the Japa goes on, with complete concentration by getting deeply immerged in the throbbing of the sacred Mantras.Pranic energy in the system can be enhanced by stiffening and tightening of the body or body parts and the relaxing couple of times, and then diverting, thus accumulated energy to the navel centre, which is transformed into the Udana prana. Furthermore, just by creating vacuum in the system i.e. expelling trapped air from the system, Udana prana can be generated and then increased by taking the fresh breath.

From this navel location, this Udana Prana needs to be taken mentally to the Muladhara chakra and its presence is to be physically felt there. Udana Prana on reaching the Muladhara chakra is known as/or termed as the life force. This life force awakens the dormant three and half inch coiled Kundalini. Life force with Kundalini from here through coccyx via Sushumna Nadi tends to move upward gradually by the years of spiritual sadhana/ practice and by the grace of guru and one's own past good karmas. By its vertical movement, it tends to pass through the Swadhisthanam, Manipura and travels to Dhahara /heart chakra. Further, it moves through Visuddhi chakra where life force gets purified and then passing through Lambika chakra, it reaches at the Ajna chakra as the divine light. At Ajna chakra, the point between the eyebrows, the Udana Prana/life force /divine light is concentrated. Its concentration for long duration is really very difficult. It is like holding the wind without enclosures and having no boundaries. But by regular practice and God's grace, gradually Sadhaka finds that duration of its concentration increases as the divine light passes through the Akula chakra. From this location, after a long practice, transformed divine light moves upward towards Sahasrara and most of the mental energy/residues, which could not be transformed into the divine light, stays back at Ajna Chakra.

The life force on passing through Dhahara/heart center carries with it by its magnetism, the pure tiny human soul/Jeevatma, which rests at Dhahara chakra. It is much less than the size of an electron and it is irresisistibly drawn to the life energy, up to the Ajna chakra, till it arrives at this Ajna Chakra center. Here the soul rests after getting purified at the Visuddhi and Lambika chakras. The Jeevatma tries to leave and forget all its horizontal plane problems/issues while resting uninterptely without any thoughts at Ajna chakra. The human mind tries to get dissolved in the soul or gets separated from it at this location. It turns into pure sensation without any thoughts and thoughtless stage is achieved at this junction. At this stage rate of breath is also minimized. Basically it is breathless and thoughtless stage. Breath basically gets suspended at this stage. If this stage at the Ajna chakra is achieved and Ajna chakra is sufficiently energized, the life force turn gradually into divine light and Sadhaka just becomes root, the Jadah without chetna/ consciouness. The life force after turning into pure light takes the vertical sky travel, and adopts the pathless path. Thus light travels upwards through Brahmnadi and gradually by its own by the grace of Almighty; it travels vertically up to the Unmani. At Unmani it turns into purest light and on taking further vertical pathless path, it penetrates Sahasrara chakra, thousand pedal lotuses, on a way to merge with the Supernal. This is a highest blissful stage. It merges with the Supernal light and comes/returns back to Unmani chakra. It is a stage of Savikalpa Samadhi. And this process goes with awareness and at times without awareness of the Sadhaka/aspirant. If by the God's grace it merges and does not come/return back, it is the Nirvikalpa Samadhi. Generally, while alive and attached to the gross body in a human life, Sadhaka is blessed by Savikalpa Samadhi. This can be for a few seconds to maximum of three minutes. It is a blissful stage as if river water is merged in the ocean and by the force of ocean waves, water is pushed back into the river, and this divine process goes on, as and when a Sadhaka is in deep meditation. The return/pushed backwater to the river is now the mixed water containing graceful sweet and salty texture of divine nature. It is like a threshold of Jeewan Mukta stage and is a very mystical and personal Anubhuti/experience of the advanced Sadhaka/aspirant. However, upon leaving the body at the time of death, Sadhaka takes Nirvikalpa Samadhi by His grace and become Jeevan Mukta—the free from bondage of birth and death.

2.2 What is the benefit for revolving the life force through all the charkas number of times through the Sushumna Nadi in the spinal cord/system?

By the grace of Almighty in the process of Yoga Sadhana, Udana Prana is generated. This Udana Prana, which is later called or named as life force, by the years of sincere practice, passes through the Muladhara chakra via coccyx and gradually ascends through the spinal cord via Sushumna Nadi to the Ajna chakra. After piercing through Swadhistanam, Manipura, Dhahara/Anahata, Visuddhi and Lambika chakra, this life force gets settled at the Ajna chakra, which is Kutakasha Chaitanya center. It is located in between the eyebrows. Life force energy gets concentrated at this center/chakra. It is two pedals chakra. Here at this chakra, life force either can take vertical path or take the backward path to the Muladhara. It is very important center. It is gateway to Chida Akasha and the highest center for monitoring and controlling the horizontal plane activities. By the self-efforts and Guru kripa/directions, one can ascend the life force at this level. Above this is the pathless sky path, life force/light move itself through Braham Nadi by the blessings of the Almighty/Cosmic Mother.

At this chakra, after deep concentration on passing through Awakening, Dreamy, Susupati and Turiya stages, the life force gets transformed into the Cosmic divine light and ascends through vertical sky path by Brahamnadi to the Chida Akasha gradually and on passing through the nine charkas on this sky-ness path, it reaches to Unmani chakra before piercing through Sahasrara chakra on the way to the mergence with the Supernal. If the life force cannot transform in to light due to various unforeseen reasons, it takes the downward journey from the Ajna chakra back to the Muladhara passing through Lambika, Visuddhi, Anjana, Manipura and Swadhistanam charkas. Sometimes with the fastest speed it reaches to its starting origin i.e. Muladhara. Sometimes, it looks as if through astral plane the life force has descended. It can also ascend through the astral plane for the advance Sadhakas. For the life force to follow the vertical sky-ness path depends on the evolution of the Sadhaka and his years of long practice along with the grace of the Almighty.

During descend, the life force likely to follow the same backward path and thus completes the one round of revolution in the human system from Muladhara to Ajna chakra, and Ajna to Muladhara. Again by the presence of lively pranic force in the life force, and by deep mental inward concentration or by the advanced breathing exercise of the Kriya yoga, it can again ascends/climbs up through the spinal cord like a serpent via Sushumna Nadi, and on passing through the various charkas, reaches with the least resistance up to the Ajna Chakra. It stays there for a few seconds and Sadhaka enjoys the presence of Shakti at the Kutaksha Chaitanya center before it takes the backward descend path. The mind of the Sadhaka with this process of the movement of life force gets fully inward engrossed within the life force and its upward and downward movement in the spinal cord. By repetition of this process again and again in the spinal cord, the Sadhaka experiences that the total energy of the system is concentrated in spinal cord and particularly in the Sushumna Nadi, and quanta of energy is moving up and down between Muladhara and Ajna and back. In this way, Sadhaka feels that all other major system of the body including heart, lungs etc. are fully relaxed during this process since the energy has been withdrawn from the entire system and has got concentrated in the vertical spinal column. It is basically Jada and Achetan/unconscious state for the Sadhaka for the outward happenings around him since the energy from all the five senses have been withdrawn. Under these conditions /status, there is no energy with the ears, eyes, nose, skin and tongue, and the master of energy—the mind is engrossed and enjoying the movement of the energy in the spinal cord. This is the stateless state of the Sadhaka although mind still being in a horizontal plane up to the level of Ajna chakra, he is in a state of full relaxation. In this state, no physical movement of any part of the body is taking place and complete system is stand still except auto system of the body, which is in the working mode and complete energy of the entire system is concentrated in the Sushumna Nadi. Mind is in the Thoughtless, Silence, but conscious State with the inward awareness of the pranic life force energy.

As the life force travels up and down through the Sushumna Nadi, it magnetizes the Sushumna Nadi since life force is an Udana

Prana—a concentrated quanta of the pranic energy. Its repeated up and down movement through the Sushumna generates the electro-static energy on its tiny walls, and gradually the walls of Sushumna Nadi becomes magnetized since the Sadhaka during Yoga Sadhana is insulated from the feeble magnetic fields of the earth by insulating himself from the earth by using the insulated carpet/cloth on which he sits for meditation. Once the Sushumna Nadi is fully magnetized, the magnetic charge energy gets transmitted to the spinal cord by mutual induction process, and thus, the spinal cord gets magnetized. Since sun and moon nadis (Idla and Pingala) are the important parts of spinal cord and are housed in it, also get magnetized during the process along with the other Nadis of the spinal cord. In this way each and every cell of the spinal cord gets magnetized. Gradually, number of spiritually magnetized cells increases and also the concentration of intensity of spiritual magnetic charge on each cell increases. As this process goes on, sun and moon Nadis after getting fully charged act as the main source for the distribution of spiritual charge energy to the entire system by the process of breath in and breathe out. This is because of the fact that these Nadis are closely linked with the breathing system and breathing process. It is well known that oxygen and pranic energy get distributed to each and every cell of the human system, and thus spiritual energy also get distributed through this process as the reserve of charge of magnetic spiritual energy increases in sun and moon nadis of the system. Gradually by years of practice of revolution of life energy through the spinal cord, each and every cell of the body retained the charge of spiritual pranic energy. Minimum 12 to 20 years of sincere practice may make the Sadhaka fully spiritual by body, mind, intellect and deeds. His thoughts and words will become fully spiritual. This in turn increases the mind's spiritual energy and turns the Sadhaka a spiritual enlightened Yogi. This is a process, but all this is possible by His grace since Maya—illusion will try to take him back to square one again and again. But he must get up again and again and walk, like a child until he/she learns how to walk alone without a support.

By the above practice, the body of the Sadhaka gets charged gradually with time, and even an ordinary person can feel the certain amount of feeble voltage if Sadhaka is just touched. In short, circulation of life force in the spinal cord of the Sadhaka/spiritual aspirant, turns him gradually to a perfect yogi who develops all the occult powers in due course of time. Pramahansa Yogananda Ji has clearly mentioned in his spiritual realization discourses that one round of circulation of life force through all the chakras in the spinal cord gives an evolution of one year. This means that by perfect spiritual living of one year by thoughts, words and deeds, the amount of spiritual energy, which Sadhaka accumulates in the system, one round of travel of life force from Muladhara chakra to Ajna chakra and back renders the same amount of spiritual energy to the system, and one round of this travel of life force just takes a few microseconds. Thus, Kriya Yoga leads the accelerated evolution to a devotee/Sadhaka so that in his life span itself, he can be self realized soul, can achieve mergence with the Supernal and may attained Savikalpa and then Nirvikalpa Samadhi in due course with out any restrains by the blessings of Almighty. This quickens the evolution process and one becomes spiritually realized in this birth and can become Jeewan Mukta/liberated soul by the grace of his Guru and Mahaavtar Baba Ji, which otherwise would have taken several uncounted births.

The above as discussed, is the benefit of the ascending and descending of the life force in the spinal cord in the human system. No other process can render such benefits and make an ordinary human being a self realized soul in this life span. What is basically required for this highest achievement in one's own life span is burning devotion, immense patience, rigid desire/sankalpa and above all Guru's grace and kindness & blessings of the Almighty.

2.3 Why a Spiritual aspirant/Sadhaka sometimes needs to feel like to rub his skull and Apex center during meditation when he feels the presence of the light in the Apex center under the skull?

This question is beyond understanding and apprehension of even most of the advanced Sadhakas. It is difficult to understand and appreciate this query. But those who are at the advance stage of mergence with the Supernal, for them this is an obvious question. During the process of self-experience after advancing in the spiritual path of evolution, such advanced seekers are eagerly looking forward to know the answer of this rare query. Only Satguru who himself has experienced such unusual experiences during his own process of spiritual evolution is only can confidentially answer such queries.

The answer to this query can be understood in a simple explanation like this:

Our head with Apex center with many small hairs are like the base, and roots of the giant tree/plant coming out from it, which is like an earthen pot having roots of the tree. Hairs are like roots of human body, which take energy from the atmosphere/cosmos like roots of actual plant taking energy from soil/earth, they are planted in, and feed to the branches of the tree. In the same way hairs planted in a skull take energy from the atmosphere/sky/cosmos and feed to the human system, which is like a reverse planted tree. Also, hairs can release energy after taking from the human system to the atmosphere/cosmos. Thus human hairs on the human skull work both ways taking energy from the body, releasing to Cosmos, and taking energy from Cosmos feeding to the human system. In other words human body is considered as a giant tree and hairs are the roots of the tree taking energy from soil/human body releasing to the branches/atmosphere, and taking energy from Cosmos/ atmosphere and feeding to the system.

Advance yogis in the spiritual science, can take cosmic energy from the universe/sky/atmosphere through the hairs rooted in the skull and can easily transmit the collected cosmic energy/light to the entire physical system and thus can live long and happily with the minimum use of body system/organs. Also, they can transmit subtle light/pranic energy to the atmosphere by the skull through the hairs, particularly by the Apex center as and when required. In this way advance yogis can communicate with the universe through its cosmic energy and life force/light/pranic energy of the self. And thus, such advance yogis can live without taking direct food from mouth as an ordinary human being. They live by the subtle cosmic energy. In short, communication can be established with the Cosmos by this process, and light energy can be absorbed as well as can be released to the universe as and when such advanced yogi want to communicate with unmanifested part of the Brahma i.e. with the cosmos. This is the most advanced stage of the human being. He can be in vertical plane and as well in the horizontal plane as per his wishes. This is possible because human hairs in the skull can work both ways and this faculty can be exploited through spiritual development.

Through yogic process, life force/Udana Prana after ascending from various charkas i.e. Muladhara, Swadhistanam, Manipura, Anahata, Visuddhi, Lambika (at the palate center), it reaches to Ajna chakra. It further ascends from Ajna chakra to Sahasara through Unmani chakra including 9 other chakras, whose location is not exactly known in the Chida Akasha for mergence with the Supernal via Apex center.

When light ascends up to the Unmani chakra, from here it must ascend vertically upward but some times since it is a pathless path of light in Chida Akasha, it may spread under the skull due to the lack of kinetic energy in the pranic/life force. Thus, light takes/ adopts the path of horizontally -vertical and/or vertically- horizontal under the skull. This is quite common for all those who have not frequently merged with the Supernal, and are in the initial stage of evalution. On such occasions Sadhaka, the spiritual aspirant, feels like rubbing his skull by the tip of his fingers and thus the light finds the way to Akasha/sky as the roots of the hairs in the skull get charged by rubbing and attract the magnetic life force/light, and thus communication with cosmos is easily established. This is the stage of Awakening-Turiya /transcendental, since spiritual aspirant is fully aware how the life force is moving upward towards sky. Gradually from this stage Turiya-Turiya /transcendental-transcendental is achieved automatically if Sadhaka gets absorbed in meditation for a long time in time-less stage. This is the stage of time-less consciousness.

At this stage feeling of time is diluted /disappeared.

In the advanced spiritual state, occasionally, sadhaka experiences that the cosmic light, by the grace of the Almighty, starts descending automatically from sky/cosmos from Apex center via Sahasara to Unmani and on passing through Chida Akasha after crossing various Chakras finally reaches to Ajna Chakra. Here light gets coupled with the life force, which has already ascended from Muladhara chakra to Ajna chakra. Gradually the path between apex center and Ajna charkas via Braham Nadi becomes Sahaj i.e. without any resistance, and spiritual aspirant/Sadhaka with minimum efforts can ascend to Turiya-Turiya state from awakening to Turiya state. When aspirant is able to arrive frequently at this state then only vertical path is adopted by the light, and light no more follows horizontally-vertical path and nor the vertically-horizontal path, and thus no more rubbing of the skull is needed to arrive at the final state of mergence. The path of the light for its vertical ascendance becomes Sahaj, without any resistance.

The above experiences are very subtle in nature for the path of light/energy through the pathless way in the stateless state of Sadhaka/spiritual aspirant. In short these complex queries and theirs answers/explanations are very difficult to apprehend unless one has his own experiences/anubhuties by the grace of Guru, and blessings of Mahaavtar Baba ji and the Almighty.

2.4 Why the Sadhaka/spiritual aspirant starts sometimes recitation of mantra automatically when the light tends to strike the Apex center/Sahasara chakra but unable to cross and merge with the Supernal?

This experience an advanced spiritual aspirant goes through very frequently even after having mergence experience of several times. It is quite unusual but happens and the cause of this, a spiritual aspirant, does not know. When light ascends up to Apex center but unable to strike Apex center, spiritual aspirant starts automatically praying mentally to Almighty for His assistance/grace/help. Sometimes he succeeds to strike the Apex center and finally gets mergence with the Supernal, but most of the times spiritual aspirant ends his meditation with Manta japa/recitation that happens automatically and finally life force/light descends back to the lower charkas and mind of the aspirant returns back to the horizontal plane without getting the grace of the mergence. Spiritual aspirant feels mentally unhappy for his failure but he again puts his efforts for the next sitting and accepts this as the wish of the Almighty.

Basically, the reasons for this particular hindrance for ascendance of life force/light to the Supernal are not very complex but the connections of deep-rooted issues of the horizontal plane are very closely involved. When spiritual aspirant during meditation ascends subtle energies, which are not completely integrated in unison from Ajna chakra to Chida Akasha, these energies do not comprehend the integral force and get disintegrated as it ascends. The subtle energy must be integrated light consisting of life force in which mental energy, soul vibrations, consciousness, awareness etc., and all types of energies are completely composed in a bindu/dot/point. This subtle energy point/dot must be completely cohesive, integrated and shall be like a light beam edge. But, at time, it does not happen although for a spiritual aspirant who practices regularly, however it should happen. This happens primarily due to the various issues of the horizontal plane, which remained unresolved in the mind and mind revolves around these issues and not able to come out of these deep rooted issues even in meditation. Part of the mental energy remains entangled with these issues although the mind tends to dissolve in soul at the Ajna chakra but in a subtle way entangled energy remains precipitated as the separate identity as the light ascends. Since the light dot is not completely composed and cohesive so before reaching to the Unmani chakra and/or striking Sahasara, the light get spilt with the slightest impact in its original constituents and mind, soul, awareness, consciousness, Prana and other negative mental horizontal energies get precipitated as an individual identity. This being the zone of higher throbbing, the divine Nada in the form of Mantra gets started mentally automatically by the spiritual aspirant at the highest plane under the effect of spilt light energy.

Sometimes under the effect of Mantra power or by the prayer of the aspirant all these spilt subtle energies get integrated and become as a cohesive light edge by the magnetic impact of the Mantra vibrations. And thus the light follows the original path of striking the Apex center and mergence with the Supernal. But, if the integration of the spilt energies does not take place with the continuous repetition of Mantra, various thoughts start attacking the mind. Mind from dualistic pattern turns to the multidimensional pattern and various deep thoughts of horizontal plane start pouring in the mind. And finally spiritual aspirant leaves meditation under disgust, bows before Almighty as an unsatisfied creature, repents and blame/curse himself for his failure to mergence. Sometimes, he very well understands that he did not start the journey after having resolved all the mental issues but all the same unsatisfaction prevails in his heart and mind till he accomplishes the further successful journey.

At this junction spiritual aspirant must understand the various causes of all such obstacles in the vertical path and to overcome these obstacles he must try to maintain vacuumed in his entire physical system by taking out/by exhausting all the breath/air by force from his system like a snake. A snake becomes breath-less number of times by hissing sound, as he takes out all the breath and stay in the breathless static state. A spiritual aspirant must follow this and try to become breathless by taking out all the breath by number of times like a snake. Then only it may be possible or it may be helpful to reach the integrated state of a point light edge to penetrate through the Apex center to take up the upward journey to sky/cosmos for mergence. It is only possible by the grace of Guru, Baba Ji and by the blessings of the Almighty. All efforts of the Aspirant are secondary.

If the spiritual aspirant does not succeed by all his efforts as discussed above, he need not abundant/leave his efforts for the upward journey but must continue in the next sitting, and accept such failures as a part of the stride for the spiritual evolution.

2.5 What is divine romance? And where does it lead?

Liking of one another finally leads to love. When couple loves each other to the extent possible then they cannot live without each other, this brings them to the final stage when they want to merge in each other that lead to the stage of romance. Basically romance is higher and respected version of love. Romance is not possible, rather it is futile without the intrinsic linkage of delicate love. Romance without love is a lust. And lust turns into hatred, breakage and separation in course of time. Love is the source of successful physical romance in the horizontal/worldly plane. On the physical plane love between the couple is a gateway to romance otherwise it is the process to deplete the vital energy that makes the self gradually physically and mentally sick without getting the glimpse of satisfaction, and to be in a state of unison, and be in a blessed state, which is the net outcome/resultant of meaningful/ successful romance.

Love is at the threshold of romance. What is love? it must be understood in depth? Love is not just kissing, hugging and speaking just a few sweet words under the effect of lust and then quarreling and exchanging the unpalatable words. Love is the nectar that gives pleasant aroma and attracts the couple to merge in each other and forget themselves in totality becoming one to live in unison in physical, mental, Pranic/subtle and spiritual planes.

Love is gross but romance is subtle. It is not merely a feeling as love brings. It brings all that cannot be described and expressed in words. All words and language become futile to project the glory of romance. One can handle and look at the flower, can feel and smell the presence of its pleasant aroma, but unable to preserve its aroma by any available means. So is the romance that is like aroma of the flower, beyond the expression by the words. It is a pleasant mental feeling. Whatsoever one describes, he is unable to express the pleasure and happiness as the net blessed effect of the real romance.

On the contrary, "LOVE" by its literally word meaning can be understood as: "L" for listening, "O" for observing, and "V" for venture, and "E" for evolution. So if couple loves each other, they will listen to one another and try to move in unison in all aspects.

They will physically and mentally "observe" each other very closely and also try to venture in each other happiness and sorrow, and finally both of them try for higher evolution in course of time. And thus enters as a causeless couple to the state of intrinsic romance and get absorbed in each other like an Ardha-Nareeswara.

For the multiplication of species, Almighty has created swarup/ image of Kameshwara and Kameshwari that act as the instruments inducing desires to couple to multiply their species. It starts from physical and mental attraction that proceeds in love and ends up in romance. The romance may end without much pleasure if coitus of any of the partners is premature. But if the coitus of both the partners is simultaneous, then the couple just forgets each other both in mental and physical plane. Both the partners merge in each other as milk in water and become one as if in unison. This is the stage of romantic Samadhi in the horizontal plane until both are again conscious of each other with time. That timeless state in unison is the period of Samadhi/trancendental state. These few moments are like mergence of Shiva and Shakti and appearance of bindu/dot after both have disappeared in totality. It is the blessed outcome of the romantic state. If both of them experience this in coitus, their love, understanding and oneness increase in all walks of life. Their thinking in any work, their feelings, their way of approach in any crucial critical matters will always be identical as if they are made for each other on this planet. Romance for them is not the sex but the mergence to be in unison. The process of romantic act continues as if Shiva is merged into Shakti, and finally the nectar of their romantic divine love gives the fragrance to the flower that appears out of their union. And this aroma will be filled with all virtues, and in short the blessed soul that appears, will be Sampuran Guna Sampan i.e. he will be highly evolved soul. This is the valuable gift of the divine romance in the horizontal plane. It is not the by product of the desired/undesired sexual activity of the couple. This is the priceless gift from the Almighty, and couple will realize this in course of time.

On the similar modes as above if the spiritual aspirant loves the Almighty, only then divine romance appears in the intrinsic heart of the Sadhaka. This divine romance gradually merges the soul of the spiritual aspirant with the Supernal. This happens with the grace of the Almighty. The soul of the Sadhaka after taking the nectar from the Supernal on getting merged, returns back to the Ajna chakra, rests there for a few seconds and again ascends, and get merged with Supernal, and thus draws cosmic energy from the Supernal. This is the highest achievement of a spiritual aspirant in his life. This divine romance of soul with the Supernal continues and Sadhaka becomes unaware of this divine play with time and this timeless stateless state of the spiritual aspirant is called Savikalpa Samadhi that takes his soul to the state of Self-realization. This is the highest success in the life of a spiritual aspirant. In short, the divine romance is the pathless path of the soul for mergence with the Supernal that leads to Savikalpa to Nirvikalpa Samadhi gradually. This happens when the soul becomes the part of Supernal like water in the milk, and return back from this highest state of Nirvikalpa Samadhi by the wish and grace of the God. He then becomes Jeewan Mukta /liberated soul in this life. This is the highest degree of divine romance and there is no comparison what a spiritual aspirant achieves in this romance as nectar of divine blessings from the Cosmic Mother.

Prior to the highest degree of divine romance, a spiritual aspirant after years of spiritual Sadhana achieves glimpses of divine love when life force of the aspirant ascends from Muladhara Chakra to Ajna chakra and descends back from Ajna to Muladhara. One such revolution of life force in the spinal cord is the first step of feeling of divine love. Mergence of life force at the Ajna Chakra for a few seconds and then its return path to Muladhara Chakra, and thus continuation of this back forth journey of life force and its stay at Kutastha Chaitanya Centre/Ajna Chakra is the mergence feeling of spiritual aspirant in the highest divine love. This whole is a divine love process. At times tears start flowing from the eyes of the aspirant out of divine intrinsic love for Almighty. Sadhaka basically forgets every thing in this process and his complete physical and mental energy from all the sense organs get concentrated in the spinal cord and ascend and descend of the life force continues through the Sushumna Nadi of the spinal cord. In this process spiritual aspirant feels the highest order of divine love in the stateless state of timeless scale.

The transformation of life force to the divine light occurs at the Ajna Chakra when all the mental forces merge in the soul. Here aspirant passes from awakening state to Dream state to Susupati before entering to the Turiya/trancendental state. On passing through Turiya state life force change to divine light and ascends to Chidakasha. In the divine light, there is no mind, no intellect, no Chit and no awareness/Chaitanya It is pure bundle/quanta of light energy, and if Supernal light from cosmos via Apex center descends and meets with the soul divine light ascending upwards then there occurs the unison of Shiva and Shakti in the Chidakasha between the Ajna chakra and Sahasrara. The Supernal cosmic light being Shakti, and soul divine light being Shiva and their mergence in the Chidakasha is the blessed divine romantic mergence state in the head of the Sadhaka. There is no bliss beyond this that an aspirant can experience. This divine romance continues as make and break circuit till the soul divine light becomes the complete part of the supernal light. At this state the aspirant is in Samadhi—a stateless timeless state. In this state complete knowledge just pour in and nothing more remains to know and learn.

This highest divine romance charges the complete physical system, mind, subtle system, nervous system of the spiritual aspirant and he fully fills himself with infinite blessings of the Almighty. In this state of divine romance, an Avadoota/spiritual aspirant can sit for a long time and goes on accumulating the divine light and in this stateless state of romance he becomes fully enlightened. But he is unaware of his enlightenment and he just cannot discuss his enlightenment unless and until Almighty gives him glimpses to talk about the divine knowledge and the process of enlightenment.

A spiritual aspirant of divine romance can go to trance any time. He is the complete master of his senses. He has full control on his mind since he is always with the light when he is in divine romance; his energies are always in the higher spiritual centers. No horizontal desires can provoke him. He is without any Vasanas/desires. Aspirant has always good thoughts, positive thinking and he is always engaged in creative activities for divine cause and human welfare through divinity. Erotic romantic thoughts of horizontal planes are far away to disturb him. He is living divinity and close associate of the Almighty and can take dip any time in the divinity of the Cosmic Mother.

In short, a spiritual aspirant in divine romance becomes divine personality and gradually turns in to divine light by the blessings of his guru, Mahaavtar BabaJi, and by the grace of Almighty. This is the highest achievement of spirituality of the spiritual aspirant—the Sadhaka in the human form.

2.6 From Visuddhi Chakra onwards, what path the life force/ divine light must follow for mergence with the Supernal for a spiritual aspirant/Sadhaka to be in a blessed state?

This question is very significant and pertinent for the advance spiritual aspirants/Sadhakas since the Udana Prana/life force is full of vitality and finds its path towards Muladhara, and from there to other higher centers after a few years of practice and has tendency to go straight to the Apex center after crossing Visuddhi Chakra and Ajna chakra. From Apex center it can ascend to cosmos in the awakening mode and also can roam in different planes, in different directions and can descend back to Apex center, then to Ajna chakra and after this it is to settle in the Muladhara. It seems when it goes straight to the apex center as if the soul with the mental energy along with the life force has gone for excursion in the cosmos and returned back without any spiritual gain and without experiencing blessed state in the complete process. Of course, it is much advanced and superior state, and no doubt a very subtle achievement in the life of a spiritual aspirant. But what is its purpose? Does it serve really any meaning of being spiritual aspirant? However, even to achieve this stage Sadhaka spends a major part of his life.

An appropriate advance spiritually realized guru/master can only advice to the spiritual aspirant that this is not the path to be followed in the pathless path in the stateless state for the spiritual advancement to get into the blessed state. An advance guru can only make him understand that following this path will give the aspirant only the pleasure of cosmic excursion but not the spiritually advanced blissful state, which is the purpose of spiritual realization. The soul that follows this excursion path to the cosmos is the Prataksh Atma and not the pure soul light. It is the soul with Jeeva. No spiritual evolution takes place in Sadhaka since the light/life force following this path does not pass through Brahmnadi to Sahasara to Apex center and then to the Supernal. Without passing through Brahmnadi to Apex center, divine light cannot couple with the Supernal, and cannot enjoy blissful state being in void and will be without visual experiences.

The spiritual aspirant must be very vigilant in the initial stages of spiritual development that from the Visuddhi chakra onward life force must pass through Lambika chakra before reaching to Kutastha Chaitanya. Here at the mid point between the eye's brow i.e. at the Ajna chakra, life force must get concentrated and whole mental energy of the Sadhaka must get submerged in the spirit/the pure soul. At Dhahara chakra only pure soul must ascend with the life force leaving behind the Jeeva otherwise spiritual aspirant may get lot of visual experiences at the Ajna chakra onwards. Mind must get fully merged with the soul at this center and then soul must step into the dream state to Sushupati state i.e. deep slum state. The complete kinetic energy of mind must get transformed into the potential energy at this point. The spiritual aspirant gradually must come into Turiya/ transcendental state at this location. Then life force under these conditions turns into the divine light and by divine awareness it ascends upward taking the pathless path towards sky. From this location gradually by divine blessings, it reaches to the Unmani chakra passing through Brahmnadi crossing other nameless 9 chakras in the Chidakasha. As a pure light it ascends without mental energy merely by partial divine awareness. This divine light by it self penetrates the Sahasrara— the thousand pedal lotuses before reaching to Apex center towards its way to the Supernal, and the spiritual aspirant enjoys the divine bliss when the pure light soul merges with the Supernal. On the contrary, if this path is not followed, Sadhaka cannot enjoy the blissful state. So the spiritual aspirant must be very vigilant that the life force must be concentrated at the Ajna chakra before it ascends further as the pure quanta of divine light. Similarly if the cosmic energy is descended to the Apex center from cosmos, it must be allowed to be concentrated at the Ajna Chakra, and then gradually it must be allowed to descend to other downward charkas through the spinal cord.

The traveling of life force to the Muladhara chakra and then to the higher centers continues till the sufficient energy/life force/ light is accumulated at the Ajna chakra that can automatically ascends upwards towards sky/cosmos to merge with Supernal by the inbuilt divine force in it. This can lead the spiritual aspirant to Savikalpa Samadhi. On the contrary Prataksh atma/soul cannot lead to Savikalpa Samadhi. Prataksh Atma can only take up journey to cosmos and return back to Apex center without any spiritual enlightenment, without entering the zone of perfect silence. Savikalpa Samadhi and Nirvikalpa Samadhi state can only be achieved if perfect divine path of ascend is followed through Ajna chakra onwards. This only can enhance divine qualities in the spiritual aspirant and can gradually turn him to be more compassionate, sincere, full of patience & kindness, truthful, to increase in him the quality of forgiveness and so on and transform him to a divine personality of universal love. He then cannot hate any body and not even his worst enemy.

In short, the path which divine light follows is much more significant for spiritual evolution of spiritual aspirant then merely roaming of Prataksh atma in the sky as the visitor without any transformation in the causal and subtle bodies for any further evolution.

Chapter 3

Mind, it's Location in Human Body and Means to Control it

3.1 What is mind, where is it located in a human body/form and how does one ultimately control it?

It is very complex to answer since it is beyond logic and apprehension. There is no available literature, which discusses the location of mind in the human system; however, ways and means to control the mind have been discussed in details. In fact, the specific location of mind in the human system is still a great mystery. Modern science claims that the mind is located somewhere in the brain and based on this assumption, various techniques to manipulate and control the mind have been discussed and implemented in the field of psychiatry and psychology. However, to willingly direct the activities of mind is still a most difficult and complex proposition and the very sensible aspect regarding the mind control have not been understood. It is like trying to control the wind without adequate boundaries. One can suppress his mind temporarily, make it sleepy and functionless by help of tranquilizers affecting the brain, but to active/genuine control of mind is the most difficult activity of the human race from the time immemorial. Self - control is the mind control and key to mind control lies in the sense-control. It is said, one who has control on his mind, has conquered the world.

Before going in details of various aspects of mind control, its function and its location in the body, let us first try to understand the verbal, word and each letter meaning of the word "mind". In the word 'mind', 'm' stands for 'Maya'—the illusion, "i" stands for 'indulgence', "n" stands for 'noise', and 'd' stands for 'diversion' and 'distress'. So, literally word meaning of the mind can be expressed as:

"That sensitive instrument in a human system which indulges in Maya—the illusion, through the senses, getting engaged in time bound activities that create noise in the process, and disturbance on accomplishment; the diversion and distribution of which finally results in distress".

Mind is Maya-the illusion. Maya-the illusion is mind. Maya is Brahma so Maya is very powerful like Brahma and it cannot be controlled merely by any human efforts, means and ways. So, the mind being illusion; the Maya; is a very powerful instrument, which is capable of creating a great distress of such a high magnitude that can completely deteriorate the human system and make it functionless. So, by simple horizontal human efforts and means, mind of a human being cannot be controlled. Various means of medication and psychotherapy can suppress the mind or make it temporarily sleepy, withdrawn, and functionless. However, as soon as the effects of drugs and hypnosis wear-off, mind has the capability to draw more energy from the system, which can make him more and more violent, stronger and more rejuvenated than ever, and it becomes difficult to control it subsequently by all mundane means. By medicines/drugs, in fact, it becomes more vulnerable and difficult to control with time.

So, what is to be done to control the mind? This needs to be very clearly understood and practiced. Since mind is Maya and Maya is Brahma. It is very clear that a human being with his limited capacity and capability cannot control Brahma –the creator of the universe, since it is the part of Brahma, so the Maya and also the mind can not be controlled. From this it becomes very vivid that by any horizontal means mind, i.e. Maya i.e. Brahma, cannot be controlled. It can only be temporarily suppressed. As by closing one hole of the container, the one of the other holes may get violently opened up by increase of the pressure in side. It is the case with mind. It will jump from one point to another. It becomes clear from this picture of the mind that if some body really wants to control the mind by sincere and honest efforts after understanding real monkey nature of the mind, then he needs to follow vertical divine path in place of horizontal worldly path. This will have double benefit, firstly the mind will get controlled since much more mental energy will be utilized for vertical travel, and secondly the mind will get merged in the soul losing its individuality, and soul as pure light adopts the pathless path to the Supernal.

The spiritual science of mind control requires an understanding of the unstable, Mayavik, and dynamic nature of the mind. Mind takes energy for its dynamic nature from the food apart from the breath. So, to control the mind on the physical horizontal plane, it is required that food must be consumed in regulated selectively and controlled manners and breath must be fully in control. Precisely speaking, food must be pure and Satvik so that mind must get only Satvik and pure energy and not the Tamasik and Rajasik energies from pungent, putrid, violent — non-vegetarian food. Satvik vegetarian food gradually increases Sato-Guna and keeps the mind cool, pure and with much less of irritation. Animal-like ferocious tendencies of the mind get subsided and in turn it helps the mind to be at rest and gets concentrated easily. Not only the gross food but the food, we take from other senses i.e. from eyes, ears, nose, skin must be kept pure, it means our senses must intake Satvik vibrations i.e. we must see good in all, hear/listen good spiritual topics, smell good/fragrant items such as flowers and be in contact with the good, pure, Satvik and divine people. Directly and indirectly these activities will help the mind to control the senses, and in turn mind will get controlled easily.

Apart from various senses and gross food, mind gets subtle energy from breath. In fact, mind requires energy from the breath at all times in order to survive/exist. Mind becomes functionless if a human being becomes breathless. If the breath is controlled, the mind is under control. Breath and mind functions are very closely related. If breath is made tranquil, the mind can be kept under vigilance. Under this stage of tranquil breath, mind is always under control. Increasing the awareness can also help to manifest vigilance on mind. Awareness of mind is Shiva constituent of the cosmos; where as the mind itself is Shakti constituent— the power of the cosmos. By increasing awareness, we are better channeling the flow of Shakti and reducing noisy and flickering nature of mind. In short, if one really wants to control the mind, he has to be vigilant from all multi-directions but still the mind can jump at the earliest opportunity. Mind is just like a wind. Wind cannot be controlled, only if its energy is transformed, it will become less violent, so is the case with the mind. In nutshell, all the above worldly horizontal positive efforts can make the mind less and less violent but cannot control it fully. In the process of breathing cycle, when breath is in, a human being is active with full energy, but when he exhausts/ takes out the complete breath from the system, for a micro/nano second in each cycle, he is temporarily breathless during this interval. At this instant of temporarily breathless state, he/Jeeva is with the Supernal unknowingly. If this period is extended he can contact the Supernal. It means at every breath cycle, a creature is with the Almighty for a micro/nano second or so. A creature without breath is dead, so he dies once in each breath cycle and again revives as he takes the breath in, and thus a human being remains without mind for that short interval when breath is out of the body and fresh breath is not taken, since without breath energy human system is dead and functionless and so the mind.

Here lies the key, if a human being is able to increase this duration of being without a breath, he can put his mind more and more under control for a longer duration making it actively functionless, thoughtless, and in a state of complete rest for a number of times he breaths per minute. Less number of times in a minute if one breath, more will be his life span, and his mind will be much more in his control as compared to an ordinary being. An ordinary man takes approximately 21600 times breath in 24 hours. One can easily reduce this number by 40%-50%, and comparatively increase his life span with less of the physical problems. In other words, a void inside the system, Shuniya, vacuumed inside the system; by less number of breaths per minutes and increased in duration without breath; keep the mind under more and more control. This is the basic and easiest way to control the mind and to increase the life span to some extent.

Furthermore, to understand how the mind can be completely controlled, one must know root location of mind in the human body/system. As discussed above the human mind is like a Maya-the illusion; and Maya is everywhere in the body and around us. So, the mind is everywhere in the body and it is a part and parcel of Maya (omnipresent illusion). Thus the mind is diffused through out in every cell of the system and is also everywhere around us, in this world, in this universe, wherever, a human being wants to divert/take it. In no time, with much more than a speed of light, it can reach/touch every part of the body, can go anywhere, and can also present in various locations simultaneously. It is omnipresent like Maya, but its basic location/root is at the Brahamstanam—at the Ajna chakra – the point between the eyebrows. From here, it can go anywhere, in any part, so it looks it is present everywhere having being present no where.

Perfect control of the mind is achieved only by its mergence in the soul i.e. the self. When it gets gradually merged, frequency of thoughts occurrence in the mind becomes less and less and wandering of the mind is diminished. Thus in the process when it merges completely, the breath becomes still and the mind instantaneously disappears. Then only a perfect blissful and peaceful state pours in.

As the life force ascends from Muladhara to Ajna chakra, it carries by magnetic pull along with it the Jeevatma/soul from the Dhahara/Anhata Chakra through Visuddhi and Lambika Chakra up to the Ajna chakra, located in between the eyebrows, which is the root location of mind. The human soul rests at this point and the mind gets merged in the soul gradually by concentration. Slowly all duality of the mind disappear; mind along with soul turns into pure light. The human soul and mind at this location passes from awakening to Dreamy state and then to Sushupati and gradually to Turiya/transcendental state when the life force gets fully transformed in to pure light. Gradually this pure light travels upward to Chidakasha with slight awareness and goes through Unmani chakra to Sahasrara –thousand pedal lotuses, before mergence with the Supernal. The mind is completely disappeared/dissolved at this stage. Under such conditions, there is no breath, no mind, and no duality and thus the mind is transcended and the Sadhaka reaches to the perfect state of silence. This is the state of Savikalpa Samadhi.

This may be Jagrik/Awakening Savikalpa or Turiya Savikalpa and may be Jagrik –Turiya and so on depending on state and percentage of mergence of mind with the soul. But, it is the state of silence, without active mind and breath. Sadhaka is Jada/achetan state without awareness and consciousness. A Sadhaka can remain at this stage maximum about 3 minutes. This can only be achieved by the blessings of Almighty, grace of Sri guru/master and Mahaavtar Babji. After this, descending journey of light follows and gradually awareness and presence of mind is felt as the light reaches at Ajna chakra. From Ajna chakra to Apex center, it is a pathless path of light.

But now after descending the light after mergence, the mind gets separated from the soul gradually, but it has now changed permanently. Now the mind is no longer the original mind bound in the Maya as it was before the ascendance took place. The mind after mergence with soul becomes pure, perfectly calm without any prejudices, reactions and irritations. After the ascendance, coming back to horizontal plane it has become from small to big, great and greatest mind. Frequent mergence of mind with soul, soul's ascendance to Supernal and its descend from Apex center makes it easily controllable by the Self, actively calm, concentrated and makes it more capable of taking complex and complex creative work of the world. Human being can put his sincere efforts for all this but finally success is in the hands of Almighty and mercy of Sri Guru. Let us pray for His grace and mercy.

Chapter 4

Fate and its Control

4.1 What is fate? Can one's own fate be controlled by efforts if so desired?

Fate is indeed very complex to understand and also much more complex to define. What is stored for us in future, and what is to happen in our life without prior indications or with prior indications, is termed as our fate. So, the fate, which is likely to happen in future, cannot be predicated correctly by an expert or by the known existing science on this earth. At the most only probability can be indicated; what may likely to happen; but it is not necessary that the same will only happen.

If some one wants to define fate by wordily meaning and by the meaning of various letters used in the word 'fate', one can say 'f' stands for 'future', 'a' stands for 'across','t' stands for 'transient', and 'e' stands for 'episode'. From this it is very evident that fate is nothing but "Future across Transient Episode". From this simple definition of fate it is clear that future of any one cannot be predicted by any norms that correctly as the past, which has already happened. This is because of the fact that fate depends on the transient episodes/phenomenon which are scheduled/likely to happen in the future. In this world every thing is transient and moving, so which is likely to happen is governed by the transient phenomenon, and by which route and mode it happens, cannot be exactly predicted, hence the fate is always uncertain and is governed by multi dimensional factors. In short, the transient, how it will shape, even transient does not know, since it is instantaneous and temporary, then, how the predictors can forecast? Hence every prediction is just a broad guess within limitations and boundaries of science.

What path an electron takes, when emitted, cannot be exactly predicted, since the electron is in the transient state under the influence of energy. So, the fate being future across transient episode cannot be foreseen very vividly. That is the reason that no astrological science can lead us to predict the exact future. Its cause is very correct since it is based on the positions of the planets at the particular instant; the transient existing phenomenon occurring in the vast universe is beyond apprehension; and much beyond the present knowledge of the science. Broadly speaking, this transient phenomenon may influence the episode or not, cannot be precisely predicted. So, the predictions may happen to be true or not, it all depends on the transient X – unknown factor. This factor cannot be defined by any norms and by means of any known science. The scope of the X factor cannot be imagined and nor its strength can be measured. It is unknown, omnipresent, transient force, which can influence one's future even after his best efforts. This is what we name as; the fate; which is beyond our control. In spite of the best efforts, leaving no stone unturned, with full preparations and using excellent horoscopes, the failure do happen, which is ought to take place. In due course we understand that this is because of the effect of X factor. This is the transient Maya-illusion of the Eshwara-The Almighty/God. It is beyond the control of the human being and no human science is able to control it. All of us are puppet in the hands of this X factor. Neither it can be controlled and nor can be understood, so it is called "Prarabdha"—predestined. It is nothing, but fate-an uncontrolled phenomenon. Finally we have to accept it happily or unhappily. There is no choice before us.

It is clear that X-factor, the fate, cannot be controlled. How this can be handled and can be dealt with so that it gives the minimum misery; it is the secret, which need to be understood and experienced by the Guru's grace and blessings of the Baba ji.

In short X-factor, being Almighty, cannot be controlled by any human earthly horizontal efforts. After one's best effort, one must pray for the blessings of the X-factor for the success so that the unknown obstacles on the path and process shall not appear. For this the easiest way is to increase the spiritual power, to increase the spiritual magnetic force of the self, and to increase the quanta of spiritual light. Also, one must try to be with the Supernal every day, may be for the short interval, so as to get the grace of the Almighty. This will lead to minimize the negative effect by the X-factor and will give spiritual strength to the self to dissolve and face the consequences of the negative effects of the fate, to the extent possible. This may help to replace the bite of snake by an ant. Since, X-factor is very powerful, and everything of this universe is in its control. It is His grace, which is ultimate. One must bow before this X-factor, and need not blame and curse oneself that if he could have done such and such then these problems would not have come. It is all the baseless thinking of the mutative mind. What has to happen and what is predestined, cannot be mutated; only its intensity can be minimized and direction can be modulated by the wish of the X-factor. X-factor is the greatest and it governs us in totality after our sincere efforts and intentions since it is based on the effect of our net past and present karmas and their consequences of past lives. X-factor is always helping us by diluting effect of ill actions of past lives committed by us knowingly or unknowingly, and keeps us moving by saving us by the unbearable miseries. He is very merciful and compassionate and tries to help us in all walks of life giving us just the minimum misery as the reaction of our past misdeeds.

So, in short, we need not curse fate, not the self, and nor any other human being. One him self is responsible for all his miseries as the net reactions of his actions. X-factor is just executing the effect and tries to help us in modulation by His compassion. Let us pay our gratitude to this Almighty force. X-factor can only take us out from any misery of life and can save us. One must pray for His mercy without criticizing the fate, self, one's efforts and other associates involved with oneself.

Chapter 5

Stresses and Crisis of Life

5.1 How one can control the stresses due to one's own crisis in his life?

In a present modern life a person revolves around the stresses only. There is stress in every walk of life. From the birth to death one moves in and out of the stress only. But, no body in this world is above the stress. Stress has become the part and parcel of life. Even each one of us breathes in stress only irrespective of the age. Stresses due to job, wife, family, health, children education, their job, their marriage, environment, social pattern, money matters, difference in thinking/opinion, surrounded by evil thinkers, deceivers involved during interactions and various other unforeseen causes create mental stress and effect health and peaceful living even if one tries to be desire less and live in minimum worldly comforts without undue hurting others.

Number of stresses of day to day living in the materialistic world in a horizontal plane can be tackled on being selfless, desire less without undue mingling with others, still many stresses those are getting generated by vulnerable social elements, which are beyond the control of the self, and just cannot be avoided. A sincere, honest and divine person gets affected very severely and at time conditions become so miserable that he does not know what to do by his own knowledge of self-control and positive living. It is rather difficult to imagine a situation for an ordinary person who has not passed through such a trauma in his life. Furthermore, for hypersensitive person i.e. Sadhaka/spiritual aspirant such a situation becomes much more difficult and severe.

Before going for more details of the stress phenomenon, literally and wordy meaning of the stress has been defined. In the word 'stress', 's' stands for sensitivity, 't' stands for transient, 'r' stands for response, 'e' stands for evolvement, 's' for stigma and last letter 's' stands for syndrome. It means stress is nothing but a "sensitivity of a person towards transient response evolving stigma for unavoidable syndrome". In short it affects a sensitive person i.e. spiritual aspirant more than an insensitive person.

A common human being under stressed conditions is affected by high blood pressure, high blood sugar level, heart palpitation, mind irritation, sleep less ness and various other physical problems. At certain stage, the situation becomes very pathetic. Medicines may help temporarily but the system cannot be rectified unless the cause of the stress is diminished/removed. To overcome and remove the cause of the stress is beyond one's own control, and added to this sufferings due to physical disorders get aggravated. Gradually situation becomes from bad to worse. Although one tries his level best to tackle the cause of the stress/problem by one's full efforts and capacity, but to resolve the concerning stress level issues are always deeply rooted. These issues need immense patience, involvement, compassion and peace of mind besides in depth subject knowledge, assistance, positive advises and above all, the God's grace. Even if one of these basic requisites gets distorted during the process of tackling the stress concerning issues, the physical ailments get manifested and become vividly visible.

Now issue arises, what is to be done? One needs to deeply ponder on this. Basically, it is required that one must have a philosophical outlook of human life; on the problem; and on any of such related issues. It is to be clearly understood that even by being good, honest, and totally positive in outlook, the various problems and issues can come up in the horizontal plane in day to day life. This clearly shows that to be even perfectly good in dealings; in words; deeds and thoughts; is not the only requisite to lead a trouble free life in this world. Finally, it revolves around the "Prarabdha" of an individual in this life after doing his level best to achieve his goal, to tackle stress/problem and to get success in the life. At time nothing could be done and one has to suffer without his involvement in undue activity. Under such conditions, one need not to blame himself and nor his associates and friends. One must be clear that this is the outcome of his past accumulated karmas and he has to undergo the misery. It must be clear that life is a continuation. Even after death one has to undergo the sufferings in his new birth as the net effect of his good/bad activities of the previous birth. Any problem in life comes to give its effect and finally it gets resolved after giving some misery. So, the only solution is to pray God for His Blessings to get the miseries reduced because of the crisis. Prayers to Almighty under such adverse conditions give courage to the mind and tonic to the body.

The other very important step is to avoid all types of mental and bodily stresses while undergoing the trials of the miseries because of the associated problems. Physical signatures of the body must be very intensely monitored by close attention of the mind towards the body. It must be very clearly known that under the effect of the stresses, the basic systems, which get affected, are the digestive system, breathing pattern and heart pulse rate. Digestive system becomes more acidic, more acids get secreted and hence diet must be strictly controlled. Any type of acidic food must be avoided. More of such food to be consumed, which does not give acidic effect to keep the digestive system healthy. The breathing pattern should be kept tranquil as for as possible. It should be kept calm without any irritation to keep the mind under control. Breath rate must be tried to keep lower to retain the calmness of the mind. Mental stresses and bodily stresses always try to disturb the breathing pattern. So, one must be always very vigilant of one's own breathing pattern and try to make it tranquil as frequently as possible to retain the control of mind. Tranquil of the breath is nothing but the flow of air more or less equally from both the nostrils. Furthermore, it must be remembered that the mind gets energy from the breath, as do the other systems of the body. So, it is natural that only adequate energy to be given to mind, and also the energy given to mind must be pure, satvik and without any irritation. It is only possible when the breathing pattern is completely tranquil and breath rate is low.

It must be noted that with less breath rate excess of toxins gets accumulated in the system and this leads to increase the stress levels in the system. So, to tackle this problem due attention must be paid that the time taken for breath out should be more than the time taken for breath in. In other words, gradually it is better to make air vacuumed in the system by exhausting/removing more of air/ breath from the system and taking less of intake breath just to run the vital system of the body. If this is observed all the 24hrs a day during crisis then the stress levels in the system will not increase beyond the threshold level and mind will tend to be self composed. This will tend to control blood pressure, heart palpitation, acidity of the system, and sugar level in the body and so on.

Furthermore, increase of vacuum or Shunayaka (to excel trapped air) in the system improves the digestive system. Besides this Udana Prana must be increased /maintained in the system. This will add further to avoid any excitement of the system. Also, during stressful stage if Udana Prana is passed through Sushumana Nadi more frequently, this will enhance the calmness of mind and give rest to the system. Under stressful conditions to increase Udana prana and its passage through spinal cord becomes more and more difficult, but this is the only way to self control and maintain tranquility of mind. On the other hand indulgence in intoxication and use of tranquilizers to suppress the stress levels will tend to affect the mind adversely to take right decision and also tends to make the mind sleepy more frequently. The best and easier way to increase the Udana Prana in the system is to listen very deeply the Mantra being chanted mentally and/or vocally in the process of each breath taken along with the naval movement.

In conclusions it is emphasized that to control the stress levels in the period of self crisis in life, the best way is to pray for the grace of Guru, Mahaavtar Baba Ji, and seek blessings of Almighty apart from to put the best self efforts to come out from the crisis of the horizontal worldly plane as discussed above in details. The key process is to maintain vacuumed in the system and by maintaining breath in suspended state helps to be with the Almighty as frequently as possible besides using all possible ways and means to resolve the issues. All issues of the horizontal plane are time dependent and no issue is permanent but our attachment to the issues increases the stress levels, which is natural since all of us are in human form and ought to get affected by the blow of Maya-the illusion. There is no escape for any one of us. Maya has to be worshipped to gain its sympathy, and to get out of its blows and influences. Maya, itself is Brahma and is created by God. Maya itself can dilute its effect, and fighting with it only worsens the situation. However, it is effective surrendering to this Almighty force, the Maya, for minimizing the miseries in life.

In a nutshell, our sincere prayers from the depth of our hearts in the perfect silence mode, in the state of mergence with the Self, can only assist us and save us from all issues of stress and miseries of human life. There is no other perfect and absolute solution.

Chapter 6

Shwet Bindu/White Point and Rakta Bindu/Red Point, Purity of Environment and Role of Spiritual Energy

6.1 What is the basic concept of Shwet Bindu/ white point and Rakta Bindu/ red point? What is the role of spiritual energy and how purity of environment is maintained?

Shwet Bindu/ white point and Rakta Bindu/red point are the basic points/concept of the cosmic energy in the cosmos, and how this energy is involved, acts, and transformed in the universe is a mystery of the mystery. In the same way both Shwet Bindu and Rakt Bindu are very closely linked in human body and are the parts of a human physical system, and is also an unresolved mysterious mystery of the mankind. Both these points have been originated from a point known as Sada Siva, which is the point of basic cosmic energy and basic light source in the cosmos.

In this elemental sky in which our earth planet is located, there is located above this sky, another sky known as Hirayangarbha sky. There are also five more skies above the Hirayangarbha sky. The details of these skies are beyond the apprehension of present level of the knowledge of the secular science, and also beyond the level of spiritual existing knowledge of human being.

The divine light by the wish and desire of Almighty has appeared in these infinite skies located beyond the elemental and Hirayangarbha skies. Gradually this divine light has descended to lower skies namely Hirayangarbha sky and elemental sky of our planet from the infinite skies. This divine light descends in quanta of energy. In the time frame during travel of infinite distance by quanta of light, various different quanta of light got integrated in light bundles by the adhesion process of the quanta of light. And gradually these light bundles led to the formation of various planets in the elemental sky. In this way various planets and innumerable stars have appeared in the sky; some are smaller in size and some are very huge in size. These planets by the mutual interaction start revolving around their own axis and move in the elemental sky in a very systematic pattern.

By the rotation of these planets around their own axis and systematic movement in the elemental sky lead to have close interaction with other planets, having different heavy masses and various sizes. This generates a high frequency resonance that leads to the appearance of the electromagnetic forces of varying intensity within and around the free space of various planets. By mutual cohesion, interaction and magnetic pull among the different planets, this electromagnetic force among the planets is transformed into the light illumination energy in quanta by the different established scientific laws. This light energy partially descends to the planets located lower in the galaxy and also ascends simultaneously to the planets located at the other levels in the galaxy.

Ascending light energy takes the form of original quanta of energy and gradually returns to the five higher skies via Hirangarbha sky. Thus movement of quanta of energy up and down to the infinite higher skies is continued in timeless scale and thus different interactions are always in the endless process in the infinite time frame that lead to the formation of various planets and fragmentation of the various existing planets under the impact of the quanta of energy and its orientation. The part of light energy, which is being descended, gets spilt by the action of descending forces and divine throbbing forces existing in the cosmos by the movement of million of small and huge planets and thus the integrated quanta of energy/light points after getting disintegration take the form of Shiva and Shakti. Shiva is named as Shwet Bindu /white point and Shakti-the power is named as Rakta Bindu/red point. By cosmic throbbing both these points can join and also can spilt, and this process of integration and disintegration in the cosmos goes on as a divine play. Conversion, mergence and immergence of one into the other and vice versa continue as the divine play.

Rakta Bindu/red point is called as the Cosmic Mother and Shwet Bindu/white point is called as the Sada Shiva. These are the lords of this cosmos. By the close mutual interaction of the white points and the red points create Jeevas/creation. Also, Cosmic Mother and Sada Siva take care of their creation in this universe. The Rakta/ blood gives power to human being, and Shwet-the white points/ fluid gives vital force to human body. Thus by the interaction of the vital force of the white points and by the power of the red points jeevas are produced and get multiplied with time by the unison of the different jeevas as scientifically known process in the reproduction science. And, by the close blanket of cosmic energy / light, the jeevas/creatures are nurtured and remained healthy. The divine Cosmic Mother takes care for all the creatures for their necessities and development/growth.

By the breathing process, vital Prana/power is given by the Cosmic Mother to all the creatures of the universe that help them for functioning of all their vital organs and systems. Without this breath energy, no creature of this earth and universe can survive even for a micro/nano second. All the jeevas/creatures can survive without food, drink and other necessities for some time but not without the vital energy of the breath, which is the precious priceless gift of the divine cosmic mother to the worldly creatures.

It is very significant to understand that after utilizing the vital energy of the breath by a creature in the physical system, the distorted impure breath energy after its functioning in the system is left out as the out going breath, back into the cosmos. Thus the process of breath in and breath out is going on till a creature/jeeva is survived. The high frequency throbbing of descending pure divine cosmic light i.e. Shiva and Shakti or Shwet bindu/white point and Rakt bindu/red point, purify this impure distorted thrown out breath energy. It is purified by the close electromagnetic charge distribution of the electrons within the pure and impure energy. How exactly this happens, it is presently beyond the apprehension of the secular science and spiritual science to understand and explain in the physical plane. But one can easily imagine the worst situation around us if this pure form of energy does not exist around us and is not able to replenish the impure exhaust energy. Then the universe would be filed with virus through out, and survival of any creature on this planet would have been at stake all the time. The balance maintained by the cosmic pure divine energy is the basic secret of the survival of human race including all the creatures on this planet/earth.

By gradual increase of emission of the impure energy of the breath by the creatures, increase of the impure energy through misdeeds and evil thoughts of the human beings, the quantity of this impure destructive energy gradually increases in the cosmos. And descended pure positive energy i.e. white and red points, are not able to neutralize the available impure energy by the close nano interactions of the electrons with these energies by the electromagnetic phenomenon as discussed above. Consequently this affects the cosmic balance in various multi dimensions including balance in ozone layer. This may initiate and generate various types of catastrophes in the cosmos and universe, which will affect the normal human life on this planet – earth. This may also generate various disease ailments in the human body, and unidentified virus may appear by its own way beyond the understanding of the modern scientists. Scientists through out the world try to overcome all such problems by their own scientific way without knowing the cause of such epidemic issues. Only pure spiritual divine energy can balance this destructive impure energy of the universe, and can make the mankind healthy in all aspects including both in physical and mental levels.

A human being can best serve the cosmic mother by transmitting positive spiritual energy through his Apex center to cosmos that help an individual to be physically and mentally healthy; this makes the universe worth living by the self created spiritual magnetism; and also by transmitting this perfectly pure magnetism/life force to the cosmos to keep the balance of energies efficiently, which is beneficial to all the creatures of the universe.

In short, the lack of spiritual energy in the human being increases the cosmic unbalance of pure positive energies, and if this spiritual energy increases in general by the positive efforts of the mankind, this will automatically resolve number of problems and issues of the present generation.

Chapter 7

Mantra, Yantra and Tantra

7.1 What one should understand by Mantra, Yantra and Tantra? And what is their role in our life?

There exists lot of literature on Mantra, Yantra and Tantra, but still to define their role is very critical, and more critical is their influence on human life. There are different logics to define them but their in-depth understanding is very complex for a common man, and even for a true spiritual seeker and follower of the divine path.

Mantra is basically a divine Nada. It is a divine sound. By the ages of Sadhana, austerities/tapa, our ancient sages have perceived these Mantras/spiritual sounds directly by intuition from the cosmos, and have transmitted to the human being for their welfare. As the name "Mantra", suggests, it percolates to Mana/heart i.e. Antar Atma/inner soul directly from the cosmos by its throbbing/vibrations. Sages could identify particular Nada in their heart from the cosmos during meditation and later could produce in words. If the same words are repeated by the heart or just by vocal recitation, the same energy of Nada/sound is produced in the human mind and in his physical system, which exists in the cosmos. In other words, divine spiritual vibrations are produced by recitation of Mantra that enriches the human mind; heart and human system are magnetized and start resonating with divine vibrations. This changes the inner personality of human being gradually with time. A thief and dacoit can even become/turn into a saint. As we know the story of Valmiki who could change himself from a dacoit to a renowned saint merely by recitation of "Mara" in place of the name of 'Rama" by years of regular recitation. This shows the inner power of the Mantra. Mantras need to be recited with devotion and mind of the recite must listen it deeply and become unison with its vibrations and totally merge into it.

There are thousands of Mantras, which have been transmitted by the saints to the human beings in a span of hundred of centuries after getting merged with the Supernal by perceiving the Supernal vibrations from the cosmos in the form of divine throbbing. As for each physical problem, there exists a separate treatment and a specified medicine, one single medicine is not adequate/ to treat all the physical ailments; similarly, one single Mantra is not useful for all the individuals. Depending on the need and issues related with the different individuals, the specific Mantra is needed, which is required to be chanted in a specific way and specific number of times with full mental concentration and listening the same by getting merged in it fully. Then only the spiritual aspirant /devotee gets the Mantra Siddhi/accomplishment by the grace of the Almighty, and his desires /needs are fulfilled. Merely repeating the Mantra without mental concentration does not fetch significant benefit. By chanting with full devotion and purity of mind leads to the Vak-Siddhi / perfection of speech i.e. it means what so ever he/ devotee speaks, may happen to be true. He may achieve mind Suddhi i.e. purity of mind, which may lead to overcome the evil effects on the individual or may increase the spiritual energy of the spiritual aspirant. The developed spiritual energy can be used for various purposes besides mergence with the Supernal. This can also be used to cure the various diseases or for the improvement and advancement in the specific supernatural sciences. Furthermore, this energy can be used for the advancement in the materialist horizontal plane, gains, achieving social status/position, developing talents and so on.

The most respected and highest Mantra in all the religions of the world is AUM. It may be called Ameen, Ek Aumkar and so on in different religions, but no Mantra is equivalent to this. It creates highest spiritual vibrations in the mind and human consciousness that finally help the spiritual aspirant for mergence with the Supernal. AUM mantra can be chanted in different ways; but chanting of AUM where "A" merges in "U" and "U" merges in "M" with the prolonged sound is the most vibratory way of chanting /repetition of this Mantra. This is so powerful that this can vibrate external small lightweight items around the aspirant who chants this Mantra with intensity. All the sounds of the world finally merge as AUM.

Our breathing pattern also produces the Aum sound. This can be easily felt by just observing the breath with deep concentration. This is the only sound produced by interaction of the air revolution and its movement during chanting; and not rubbing of any organ takes place with another during this process. The final mergence of "A" to "U" to "M" leads to the bindu/point that gets transformed into the light. In other words, any divine Mantra Nada finally gets transformed into light and gradually this light travels into cosmos by years of spiritual austerities. Mantra Nada and divine light basically are the same. Both are mutated into each other when the spiritual aspirant is in deep meditation. Furthermore, AUM-HREEM-AUM is the highest mantra for the advanced aspirants that lead to merge Aum to Hreem to Aum easily, and gradually mergence of soul with the Supernal occurs with the blessing of the Almighty in a much shorter time frame.

In the spiritual science, Yantra is the other name of the physical body; the human form. In short, Mantra affects the Yantra. The recitation of Mantra creates energy that vibrates in the subtle way by its high frequency throb affecting our subtlest system of the body. By long practice and repetition of the Mantra, it becomes the part of the subtle system, and with time effect of the Mantra on the system becomes so powerful that the subtle system of the body vibrates with its refined power and various physical ailments of the body gradually vanishes. Modern science has also proved by experiments that by recitation of "Hare", "Har", "Hari", "Aum", "Shiva", etc on a regular basis for life long do not allow blockage and remove the blockage of artilleries by their subtle vibrations. This does not happen in a couple of days, but it happens only when Nada of the Mantra becomes the part of physical, mental and spiritual system. The spiritual energy generated by the Mantra recitation overcomes the entire physical and mental ailment and make the body of the spiritual aspirant full of radiance with the spiritual energy as if glory is reflected from his words, deeds, thoughts and from his face. In spiritual science such spiritual aspirant is called a man of 'Ojasav'—a divine personality; a graceful personality. The tongue of such an aspirant will speak only truth and whatsoever he speaks, will become true. The body / Yantra of such an aspirant /Sadhaka emits strong spiritual magnetic waves, and just by merely his touch, the Shakti Pada/transmission of power takes place to the fellow being. His place of sitting transmits the electro-magnetic spiritual energy that affects the aura of the people around him and transmits the spiritual energy in them without their knowledge/awareness. For some people this spiritual effect is long lasting and for some it is transient. This depends on the evolution and frequency of vibration of an individual Yantra/ body.

When recitation of the Mantra effects and influences the Yantra/ physical body of an individual by its strong vibrations to such an extent such that the subtle core of the body vibrates; then the body starts radiating Tantras——the spiritual waves by it self. Yantra/ body starts radiating the spiritual light that will be clearly reflected from eyes, body, and face of the spiritual aspirant. Even an ordinary human being can notice such a glorious reflection of the Sadhaka/ spiritual aspirant just by his ordinary glance or by coming in his contact. This spiritual light easily finds its path from the Apex center of the spiritual aspirant and merges with the Supernal automatically without creating any awareness to the Sadhaka. This is the highest state of the human being and it is called the state of Jeevan Mukta/self liberation. Thus sadhaka/aspirant becomes a librated soul even in this physical form. He comes closer with the Supernal being in the human form as per His wish. As he comes closest to Almighty; the Cosmic Mother; all his activities are executed with the closest command of the cosmic force automatically.

In short, Mantra/Nada affects the Yantra/physical body that generates and emits Tantra——the spiritual waves/vibrations that take care of every physical and mental problem; and thus he assists other human being to become perfect in all respects by the powerful effect of the spiritual energy. Tantric is the spiritual yogi of the highest order. He can easily merge with the Supernal and can control others by his divine power. Also, he can guide others to follow the divine path, and can clear all their mental doubts regarding spiritual matters; he can easily direct the divine energy of the fellow seekers in the right path for the mergence with the Supernal. This is the highest guidance that one can render to his fellow beings in this world.

The above is only possible and even feasible by the grace of self realized Guru, BabaJi, and by the blessings of Almighty.

Thus one finds that the Mantra, Yantra and Tantra are so closely related that one's life, thoughts, words and deeds are deeply influenced. One can imagine that if Mantra alone can affect the Sadhaka to such an extent, the real Yoga Sadhana coupled with Mantra along with Guru's blessings can lead to give wonderful effects within no time. And can turn spiritual aspirant, his Yantra—the physical body as a Tantric temple. This temple then can easily spreads/transmits spiritual light to the cosmos any time and can receive light from the cosmos as and when needed by the Yantra/physical body. Such an advanced Sadhaka/spiritual aspirant does not depend on the gross food for survival. His food is spiritual divine cosmic light; his breath is light that gives him all energy for survival and nourishes his body in all respects with out any ailment. He lives in light and plays with the light. Spiritual light is his companion, his guide, his wisdom and his knowledge. He needs nothing but spiritual light and always likes to merge in that light and enjoys a blissful state all the time. Such a spiritual aspirant becomes divine light/God-like in the living physical form and he is the only valuable asset in this universe and cosmos to enlighten others deserving fellow beings. Thus he becomes ocean of valuables and sky of divine light. His divine reserve of spiritual light spreads all over and he becomes source of infinite divine light.

Any follower in the path of spiritual Self- realization will like to pay his austerities to such an advanced spiritual aspirant to receive the divine light by his mere touch and blessings. In short, this is the ultimate outcome/resultant and divine fruit of the Mantra, Yantra, and Tantra along with the Yoga Sadhana that enable Sadhaka to get merged into the divine light and transmits the divine light.

7.2 What is the significance of Tantra and where does it lead?

Tantra has multiple meanings and different understandings. Tantra is the mode of vibrations with various frequencies, amplitude/energy levels of the form/body and as well as of mind, astral and spiritual body. Tantra is the particular mode of sensation of the body/mind that helps to deeply understand the mysterious secret of the Mantras, which have created these sensations.

Yantra is a symbol. It is the guide live map to reach the mysterious secrets. Human body after mergence completely in Mantra can become the Yantra, the instrument; to know the secrets of the nature. However, Mantra highlights the cause of the cosmos. It gives the secret of the beginning of the cosmos to the state of laya/mergence.

Tantra is the nectar, the Amrit Tattva. It is TAMAYA i.e. Tantra is the out come after the unison of Mantra and Yantra. Also 'T' of the Tantra, 'M' of the Mantra and 'Y' of the Yantra make the Tamaya. In other words when Mantra transforms the Yantra/the human body, and makes it as an effective tool then only Tantra is produced. Tantra is tat, the Tamaya, the Laya, the mergence. The reverse of Tamaya is Yamata (YAMATA). This depicts that "Yamata", which is unison of Tantra, Mantra and Yantra, is the final state of yoga discipline i.e. mergence with Almighty. Furthermore, without Yama, Niyama and Yoga, the mergence with self is not feasible. And without the unison of Tantra, Mantra and Yantra, the Self-realization cannot be achieved.

To achieve/reach the destination i.e. to know the secret of "Mantra", the travel/sincere efforts by the "Yantra" – the form, and the soul is required. Tantra is the ultimate soul light that enlightens and gives/reveals the ultimate secrets. SVADA and AVADA AUM Mantra take the Yantra to Para state. And in that state of Tamaya, Mantra and Yantra give enlightenment to the soul. That is the beauty and level of the Tantra. From AUM after various levels of development from ANUTA, VINUTA, KANUTA, TINUTA and AKUTA, the stage of laya is achieved. At this stage there remains no Mantra, Yantra and Tantra. That is state of SADA SHIVA-E; the state beyond of beyond. Tantra is the final state to take flight before mergence. It is the state of PRANAVA-E.

However, Tantra is Maya but it is the finest state before Maya, and before the mergence/laya. Maya is an individual consciousness till it becomes cosmic consciousness before mergence. In the final mergence death occurs i.e. in the final mergence state, death is inevitable; it is Savikalpa Samadhi, from where the return is by the will/mercy of the Almighty. This all is the play of Ishwara. Keeping Divya Drishti, in fact, only helps and gets the grace of Almighty through the Tantra, which is outcome of unison of Yantra and Mantra.

Chapter 8

Pranic Energy, Personality Transformation and Happiness

8.1 How the change of personality takes place in human being? Is it possible to achieve the stable change of personality transformation without the control of Pranic energy?

To change the personality of a person is really a very difficult task. Unless and until a person himself is not interested and fully determined to change his personality, it is not possible to bring any change in him. Personality change is purely depends on the self- efforts for a long duration along with complete determination and faith. Even if one follows the right path unknowingly for a long time, this it will modulate his personality. The concern person himself will be surprised to know all that happened to him. Scientifically speaking, causal, subtle and gross body of each one of us vibrates with certain specific frequency and with definite amplitude. There can be various frequencies in the spectrum of each body but only a few and may be one or two may be predominant. Basically these frequencies govern the behavior pattern of an individual. A person may be Satvik, Rajasik or Tamasic by nature and have different virtues of life, and this specific nature of an individual is predominantly decided by the various significant frequencies of vibration by his gross, subtle and Pranic bodies. So, in short, unless the frequency of vibration in micro and nano-scale of causal, subtle and gross bodies are not modulated, an individual remains the same throughout his life so for his thought process, life style and pattern of living is concerned.

A dacoit can turn into a saint by the modulation of vibration pattern of his gross and pranic bodies. Indian history clearly brings out that dacoit Valmiki of ancient times, who has changed himself to a saint of highest order by reciting the name of the God "Rama" as "Mara" for number of years as he was even not capable of correctly pronouncing the name "Rama". This mantra—the name of the lord "Rama" has really affected the gross, subtle and causal bodies——the Yantra of Valmiki to such an extent that gradually his Yantra, the body, started radiating Tantras—vibrations of the "Rama" itself. This has modified the personality of Valmiki in totality and in due course he could write Valmiki Ramayana—the one of greatest epics of the world that is worshipped and recited even today with highest respect by Hindus. This is indeed the miracle so for change in personality is concerned by the recitation of the Mantra. Similarly, Kalidasa, who was considered as the greatest fool through out his life, used to cut those branches of the tree where he himself used to sit, and used to fall after cutting the branches,. He could transform his personality by Mantra Siddhi and became the greatest writer; he was the author of world famous classic "Shakuntala". In our time Mahatma Gandhi could change his erotic personality from his young age and could become "Mahatma" in the ripe age. He could liberate India by following the path of Truthfulness and Non-Violence by merely his mental power. He could mobilize the masses by his selfless activities. His book "My Experiments with Truth" is the significant contribution after modulation of his personality with time along with various other contributions including "Not by Bread Alone".

Now the basic question arises how the transformation of personality takes place? By horizontal means such as adopting self control; restrains of all kinds; by different forceful means; one can temporarily affect his personality outwardly and can get some success, but within no time he will revert back to the original pattern of thinking, life style and habits. Basically the kinetic energy of a person cannot be controlled by kinetic means. Kinetic energy can only be checked, but again the resistance inserted by the will power in the path will be broken by the force and impact of the kinetic energy of original old habits, thinking and deeds and an individual reverts back to the same personality as he was. An erotic person by nature and with the inbuilt habitual inclination will never be satisfied by indulgence in sex with various women and by indefinite number of times throughout his life. A drunker cannot satisfy him self by any means although his lever gets affected. Habits are the part of the built in personality and these cannot be controlled by indulgence and nor these can be controlled by non-indulgence by will power. Habits can only be temporarily checked by horizontal means and as soon as will power is loosened, the person falls back to his original habits.

A hungry person can restrain from the food by the forceful coverage of fast or some other restraint but as soon as that restraint is over, he may jump like a hungry lion or a dog on food. One can only control him self when from inside his personality he does not really in true sense wants or feels the craving for the same. How a beggar can say that he has renounced the kingdom since he is not the king. If a king says that he has renounced his kingdom, it has significance and meaning that is indeed the real renouncement.

In short, personality change is not the outward gimmicks. It is basically an inward change in totality and it is really a very involved task that needs years of long craving and practice. By breath control, by Kumbika and by Shunayaka process, it is indeed possible to change the thinking process, and the pattern of subtle vibrations instantaneously to handle the situation at the particular moment. But as soon as the effect of Shunayaka and breath control are ceased to influence, the person resumes the same personality. However for years of practice if this pattern is really modulated, the personality change does occur. If a person is able to change the rate of breath from 16 breaths to 8 or 10 breathes a minute in course of time and if he starts breathing regularly and automatically 8 times a minutes in place of 16 times, which he was breathing earlier, then there is definitely a permanent change in his personality i.e. from rajsik personality he could change his personality to satvik in nature. Now he thinks differently, eats differently and associates with different class of people. This shows that his thoughts, words and deeds really have modified since these are the subtle qualities and have nothing to do with outward influence. The change of breath pattern has direct influence on human personality and also on one's own longevity.

To sum up it can be said with full confidence that the easiest way to change one's personality is by full Sankalpa and with complete determination as well as with the recitation of Mantra initiated by the self realized Guru; and this must be recited minimum 1.2 crore times with complete mergence in it. This is indeed a very long process but without any shortcomings, risks and drawbacks. In one birth itself one can change his personality. But the accelerated way is to go for breath control, change of breath pattern and by Shuniyaka method along with Mantra recitation. Of course in all such approaches Guru Kripa and blessings of the Almighty is the basis of success for the real achievements.

Along with the above if Sadhaka/spiritual aspirant follows the techniques of Prana control and sky ness static vision, which leads to the change of personality on burning the age old Vasanas/ tendencies, result in the fastest approaches for this achievement. In short, self determination, Mantra recitation, breath control, Shunayaka, life force/ Prana control, sky ness vision, mergence with Supernal, gradually make/turn a person with the changed personality as of a divine person who is worshipped/ adored for his achievement of divine grace in a very short span. It is basically turning a corroded piece of iron into the gold just by the touch of Paras stone, which is nothing but the God's grace by His blessings and various techniques taught by the self-realized Guru to a common deserving Sadhaka who wants to climb the highest peak of self-realization in this birth and wants to be Jeevan Mukta/ liberated soul by modulating his personality in all respects. Even if he cannot reach the highest, it must be remembered that any honest effort made by him in upward direction will positively raise him higher in all respects in this life and time to come in the forthcoming life he will certainly be God realized soul.

8.2 What is happiness and how one can achieve the maximum happiness in his life?

Happiness is a relative; for a common man it is always with respect to others; it is comparative; it is mutative; it is time bound; age bound and yuga / kal as well as generation bound; and also happiness is time, space and cause bound; and is governed by many such parameters. It is an abstract identity. It is desires bound by the Vasanas; in built tendencies, and revolves round the actions. This all shows that happiness is always transient. It is never permanent. One cannot say that he will be always happy if he is happy at this moment. Happiness is earth bound and hence it is always in motion. Happiness changes with time and age. A child can be happy with a toy but to a young man a toy cannot give happiness. And what can make a young man happy; old man happiness is miles always from that. Happiness is like a twinkling of a star. It is like a bubble that can burst in no time. But still all of us are made to look for happiness. Our whole efforts are directed towards a point that might give us happiness and that happiness vanishes like a bubble and becomes a void. Where it has got dissolved/disappeared; mind does not know; but a mutative mind again puts its affords to search for transient happiness and this game of hide and seek goes on as long as the breath is there.

We execute all our actions through efforts; through breath; since actions depend on breath and when we achieve the desired results, we become breathless temporarily to be with the happiness; to enjoy the results/outcome of happiness; but the breathless state is transient, we again start breathing to live and happiness becomes a mist in due course. In other words, in this mundane world, one cannot be permanently happy, although what so ever he achieves/gets, even if he conquers the world. His happiness is transient so far breath is there and one cannot be breathless to live to be permanent happy. So happiness is a mist, transitory, and temporary. One can run behind the happiness and it will go on shifting its center and one can go on revolving around the happiness but cannot get unless one gets dissolved in it and one cannot permanently dissolve till the breath exists. So happiness is a mysterious riddle that cannot be solved in this material world. One can go on accumulating every material thing of this world but he cannot accumulate happiness that is transient and abstract.

Happiness broadly can be divided into three broad categories i.e. physical happiness, mental happiness and spiritual happiness. In other words it is gross, subtle and causal. The gross happiness is the happiness on the horizontal plane. People look for different worldly goods and try to acquire them with full efforts to be happy. It may be house, gold, diamonds, cars and so on. Even after getting/ accumulating them, one feels vacuumed in his core of the heart and tries to get more of them; and he never gets satisfied with his desires for accumulation. This aspect may be extended to sex, power and other worldly comforts. Temporary one gets contented but again after a lapse of small interval as one feel hungry, his temptations increase and he looks to fulfill them to be happy again and again; but this well of happiness on the physical plane is never filled until and unless mind is satisfied with the accumulation of modern comforts and their frequent changes.

If the mind accumulates wisdom with age or with existing knowledge that the greatest personalities of the world have left as posterity, can assist a person for his physical, mental and spiritual satisfaction. Mind controls the senses. If a mind is made stronger from a lower to higher level, only then some direction of hope can be given to enhance the happiness. But at one stage when mind turns into the greatest mind, he can command all the five senses i.e. eyes, ears, nose, tongue and skin that look after him to fulfill his desires and get happiness out of it. In the nutshell the greatest mind only can help/assist to make a person by giving him positive direction to be happy. When intellect of a person accumulates this wisdom gradually, then happiness does not remain a mystery and person feels happy what so ever he has. It does not mean that he becomes idle, he works much more efficiently but his actions are action less and they are selfless to follow the commands of Almighty/God; and nothing for his selfish gains since his essential desires become negligible or just limited. In a simple mathematical language happiness can be defined as the number of desires fulfilled by total number of desires. So if the desires are less, the man is happy or if his most of the desires are fulfilled without increase of the desires any more. But if desires are increasing and not getting fulfilled, his unhappiness and miseries will go on increasing. He becomes miserable. So in short, the happy man is he whose desires diminish to be zero, it means nominator in the mathematical equation of desires is zero; only then his happiness is infinite. If so, then only he becomes a blessed soul.

In other words physical happiness comes with the accumulation of material goods. Mental happiness comes with knowledge; and intellectual happiness comes with wisdom.

All such happiness can supersede one and other. Intellectual happiness can supersede mental and mental happiness can supersede physical and thus higher happiness can control the lower happiness.

Basically happiness is what you are looking for. If one is looking for wisdom, wealth cannot make him happy, as Gautam Bhudha was not happy with worldly pleasures and wealth. He wanted enlightenment so he could renounce all the worldly comforts. Happiness is that which one is intending or looking for, other gains have no meaning for him.

All these happiness i.e. intellectual, mental and physical are very mutative and one can never be satisfied even having maximum of all of them. One can be really happy when his happiness approaches a blessed state of Sat, Chit, Ananda. Unless happiness is converted/ transformed into this state of Ananda/Bliss state, he will be lingering in the horizontal plane to seek some happiness or other. Blessed state is only achieved which is the mother of happiness by the control of Prana Shakti. This is possible only by being breathless i.e. by controlling the breath and ascending the life force within him and by converting this life force into the divine light. It means Maha Shuniya state of the physical system or void/ breathless can only bring blessed state when happiness is totally transformed. In this stage no desire is left. A desire less man is near to God. Man minus desire is God. It is only possible by breath control; the state of single Shuniya; coupled with Prana control; the state of second Shuniya; accompanied with sight gazing/Drishti Tratak on divine light; the state of third Shuniya. By achieving the state of these three Shuniyas i.e. in Maha Shuniya state, one can be in contact with cosmos; he can be with cosmic energy, and then only he is with the blessings of Cosmic Mother; and he is in complete blessed state and much more happier than merely with the physical, mental, and intellectual happiness.

This is the ultimate happiness. Being in this state, one is Jeevan Mukta/liberated soul. If one can get this state by Sahaj process than he is Mahayogi – the blessed soul and the happiest individual in the world just having 'no thing' but possessing every thing...

It is the state of permanent happiness and one can jump into this state as and when he wants. Being temporary – it is permanent; since it is Sahaja/easily achievable for an advanced personality.

In short, it can be concluded that happiness is transient and can be made permanent if transformed into the divine blessed state by the divine masters and by their grace. Happiness becomes a stateless state of an individual, on having every thing he posses nothing – but His/Almighty grace, which is all in all.

8.3 What is the essence of Prana and its final destination in the life span of human form? And how great heroes of Ramayana are in mysterious ways depict essence of Pranic energies and their co-relation with Pranic ascendance in the human form leading towards the mergence.

In the various earlier questions and their answers sufficient details have been discussed about the type of Pranas, their role/ interaction with the breath along with the various aspects of ascending and descending of Prana Shakti.

Now the basic query is what is the essence of prana? Broadly highlighting the essence of all types of Pranas is the Udana Prana, which can take up skyward journey. It is the life force. It is indeed very important and through this Prana the magnetic force in the spinal cord of the spiritual aspirant is developed. Its movement causes the re-orientation of energy in the human system that rejuvenates the system making it magnetic with full of divine energy.

All that is said above is very significant. But essence of Pranas is not merely Udana Prana but the light that is transformed from this Prana/life force. The transformation of divine light from Udana Prana/ life force is the main essence like ghee/butter extracted from the milk, which can be preserved for a very long time without getting spoiled under the adverse conditions of seasons and climates, where as the milk being the basis of ghee cannot be preserved for a long time. Similarly Prana/Udana Prana/ life force cannot be kept static under any location indefinitely since it is a force. It likes movement/ resolution. If it is held for a long duration at any point by force or Hathah, this may burn the cells of that location by the energy of the Prana instead of giving life to the cells, charging them with magnetic energy. But the conversion of life force into divine light illumines the entire system and manifest vivek/discrimination, intellect, peace, contentment and other divine qualities. The radiance developed on the face of the Sadhaka reflects this divine light. This divine light can be preserved in the vicinity of Apex center from where it can merge with the Supernal and descend back to the Ajna chakra from where it can take more Pranic energy and ascends again converting it to the divine light. Only the Mukhaya Prana/pure Udana Prana is transformed into light. Mukhaya Prana is the pure of the purest Udana Prana that ascends from Visuddhi through Lambika chakra to the Ajna chakra. Even from Dhahara it ascends after penetrating Ichha nadi and transforms the aspirant to Poorna Bhava State.

In short essence of different types of Pranas is the purest Udana Prana, which is called Mukhya/main Prana and its final transformation is divine light. When main Prana is fully converted to divine light the awareness of the Sadhaka gets dissolved during meditation. Light is weight less so it cannot carry any force of awareness as it ascends and moves. However, main Prana along with divine light, when it is not fully transformed, has some force and this creates awareness in the Sadhaka when it ascends to the Apex center. The awareness can be higher, lower or average but it does not allow the perfect Turiya/transcendental state. In perfect Turiya there is no feeling of breath and awareness. Yoga is not able to fuse essence of Prana fully into divine light. If it is fully converted into the divine light, aspirant enters into Nirvikalpa Samadhi. However, Sadhaka/spiritual aspirant goes to Savikalpa Samadhi for a few moments with the mixture of main Prana and light and then awareness comes after a while and the Sadhaka is back from the Savikapa Samadhi. For these moments he is in perfect blissful state and he is unable to describe since he is totally merged in that fractional moment with the Supernal. If there is perfect/ complete transformation of Mukhya/main Prana into divine light then there will not be real shadow of the Sadhaka since Sadhaka has turned to the complete light. His form becomes light, a rarefied body that cannot be projected by light and shows shadow, since body itself transmits light being divine source of light. This is a state of NISH BANDHA – the state of complete static light. It is a breathless/breath suspended state and state of complete silence. This can be simulated as the dirt and sea. Dirt has to merge with seawater but it is likely to merge slowly with time lapse but not get immediately merged. It moves with seawater before it disappears in seawater and at a distant location it looks as if dirt and sea are one. And when complete mergence takes place then this state is the state of NISH BANDHA that comes with the lapse of time although it looks very early that it has already approached. This state is basically a state of Triveni where light, Mukhya/main Prana and the awareness partially exist. All the three are bundle of light before dissolution in to the divine light. It is the combined state of earthiness with the sky ness, however earthiness will merge with sky ness with time since it is the abode of sky ness, which is a pure light. In other words it is the Divyamaya i.e. Maya in presence of subtle energy is in the mixed form of light, awareness and Prana. Gradually when this state changes to formless, oneness and nameless then only the pure light reflects and that can stay for a long time and can merge with the Supernal. To ascend to this highest state Kumbhaka at Ajna chakra is required. Trataka/concentrated gazing and Shuniyaka are the steps to ascend gradually with practice for the perfect mergence of light with out awareness and full transformation of main Prana in to the light. Here, seer, seen, seeing become one. There is absolutely no difference as if sugar has completely mixed with water so there is no sugar, no original water and not both as separate identity. Both have merged as one. This is the state of TIRUPATI BHANGA, no more trinity, all have become one.

These state of seer, seen and seeing are no more at this level of existence. DRỤG state of awareness is over. It is the state of DRUGATITA that is away from DRYASA and DRUG. This happens only when complete transformation of light takes place; and light has no awareness; and it has only Guna – the real wisdom – the divine knowledge.

Going into the depth of this subject further, Dattatraya, the master/Sarva Guru of this science has unfolded many mysterious secrets. His name "Datta" it self indicates "no more" of seer, seen and seeing that means all the three have been merged into one and in other words one has been totally illuminated. Only "ATRAYA" (derived from Dattatraya), which is immerged from "RAYA" has been left that literally means "awareness" i.e. only Apahara Karma is left after the mergence of Trinity i.e. seer, seen and seeing. It shows that after dissolution of Trinity; there is no more awareness. It is basically SAMHAR KARMA without awareness and opposite to Srushti Krama of awareness. In Samhara Krama there is "no cause" of seer, seen and seeing and so there is no residual effect of any kind. It is the state above duality. This state is above space, time and causation. It is NIRVIKALPA STATE – GARBHA STATE. When it is back with the awareness it is SAVIKALPA STATE that is stateless state back to the original state.

Further to the above there is MANON MANI that is Videha state – beyond mind and intellect; Unmani is Sushumana— a subtle state. And Ajna is Sumana state, which gives divine odor/smell.

The above intrinsic and in depth mystery gives the depth of the essence of Prana and its interaction with various states of karma, activity, inactivity, awareness and so on. Ramayana is the greatest epic of India. As a religious book of worship and its divine stories, Hindus listen with great honor and respect. But the inner meaning of Ramayana and the character of various heroes of this great epic are linked with the Pranas. A common Hindu does not understand the modes of communication of these Pranas to the different systems of the human body in depth. Knowing and conceiving this secretive knowledge is indeed the blessings to an individual aspirant since it depicts the mystery of the Pranic science and its co-relation with the Pranic ways and means in the human system that leads towards the mergence with Almighty/Supernal.

* Ramayana is the "Jagrit Agni"—— the conscious Radiant Force. Even listening to Ramayana, appreciating the characters of heroes of Ramayana, one feels the effect of Cosmic Conscious Radiant Force and wants to ascend his life as per this great epic of Ramayana.

In brief the above explanation is summarized as:

Ram

Ram as the name depicts that it is "Rama"—-- the mergence of Prana in Chida Agni. Rama is radiant force ——the Chida Agni —-- fully purified glamour radiant cosmos. The mergence in Ram Nama (chanting the name of Ram) is nothing but mergence of Prana/ life force/light with the Supernal —— the cosmic force. With this achievement/success, it is said/believed that even just by recitation of His name "Ram", all the miseries of the life is washed away/ dissolved. Ramakrishna used to go to Turiya state even just hearing or reciting the name of Rama even once. His life force always remained, rested and waited at the doorsteps of Chida Akasha/ Agni for the mergence with Cosmos/Almighty.

Sita

Sita is Janaka Raja/king Putri/daughter. As per epics she appeared while king was ploughing in the fields. This depicts that Prana comes out after traveling through Sushumna Nadi. This also indicates plug in of life force in earth Sushumna. Its appearance; coming out of Prana/life force; and mergence in Chida Akasha is the divine romance of Sita being Prana and Rama being Chida Akasha. In other words the appearance of Udana Prana in Udana/ stomach is similar to the efforts of ploughing of earth soil that gives rise the growth of plants; appearance of Udana Prana by interaction of Prana and Apana Parna at the navel centre of the human system; it is the dormant appearance of Sita—the life force/ Udana Prana, which climbs up and is merged in Chida Akasha — – Rama. So Sita is called Manu —Main — a divine beauty. She is the Vaidhya center. Vaidhai grows and climbs through Sushumana and so she is also called Sushumani. Mergence of Sita with Rama is the mergence of Soul with Supernal — the Self- realization, which is the finest goal of a human life.

Hanuman

Hanuman is the physically strongest hero of the Ramayana. In our body the spinal cord is the strongest; the whole physical body is well shaped and attached with spinal cord by various bones. Directly/ indirectly, the complete body weight is borne by the spinal cord. Spinal cord holds Sushumana Nadi, which carries and has passage for movement/travel of life force/Prank. In other words Hanuman; the spinal cord carries Sita – the Sushumani; the Prana Shakti and takes her to the Chida Akasha — the Rama for mergence with him. Basically Hanuman — the spinal cord is the bridge for retaining Sita—the Prana, and Rama — the Chida Akasha in the physical body.

Lakshman

Lakshman in the Ramayana is like a serpent; the Aadi Shesha. He always stays with Rama and Sita at their foot. He is depicted as the serpent – Aadi Shesha staying at Muladhara chakra; the lower chakra of the human body. It is the storehouse of energy; Kundilini force in the body. The Kundilini force is the food of Chida Agni/ Akasha. Kundilini force is like a servant and when ever Chida Akasha/ the master needs this force along with the pranic energy, Lakshman/the serpent/ the Aadi Shesha is released/librated by the yoga practices, which ascends and passes through Hanuman/spiral Cord via Sita/ the Sushumana Nadi and merges with Rama/ the Chida Akasha.

Bharat

Bharat is depicted as the divine Nada of the Ramayana. Movement of Pranic energy through spinal cord produces divine Nada/melody. This Nada/Bharat keeps away Vasanic tendencies/ negative forces that wanted to rob Rama Rajya (kingdom of Ram) from Rama. Bharat/ divine Nada keeps away all the evil forces from the kingdom for 14 years and handover the kingdom to Rama on his return after exile. Similarly, Nada, — Mantra force — keeps away the evil thoughts from the mind of the spiritual aspirant when the life force ascends through the Sushumna. The divine Nada — the recitation of divine Mantra helps to maintain sanctity and purity till life force after getting transformed into divine light at the Ajna chakra merges with Chidakasha.

Shatrughan

Shatrugan character of Ramayana is depicted as various charkas of the human system that act as the storehouse of pranic energy at various locations during ascend. Being the youngest hero of the Ramayana, he looks after different activities assigned to him as a storekeeper. In the human body, his role at various chakras starting from Muladhara to Sahasrara chakra is to keep the ascending energy moving; it is to fill the energy in the storehouse of the successive chakra before it is allowed to ascend further. The role of Shatrugana is keeper/preserver of the assets of the kingdom without any self-involvement and desire to indulge to rule.

Dashradh

Dashradh, the king of Ayodhaya, is depicted as ruler of 10 Pranas of the human system/body starting from Prana, Vyana, Samana, Udana, Apana, Naga, Kurma, Kurkara, Devdatta and Dhananjeya.

He controls all the Pranas of the body as the king controls the kingdom by all his forces. Prana, power and energy can be varied/ modulated as per the need of the system/kingdom by the commander/ Dasharadh—the king.

Ravan

Lastly Ravan is the head of all the 10 Indriyas/senses including Karma Indriyas and Gyan Indriyas and their functions i.e. eye, ear, nose, mouth, skin. Ravan, as the head of Indriyas and king of Lanka is similar to the head of the physical body; he is engaged himself satisfying his needs of Indriyas/senses; he takes care of all material needs of the kingdom/body. By right and wrong means he is completely indulged to satisfy them. But in a human body the material holding and their indiscriminate use never satisfy Indriyas. By greed, attachments, and committing mistakes after mistakes committed by the king Ravana; finally the Almighty – the radiant divine force – Ram— kills the king of 10 Indriyas —the Ravana to liberate the kingdom/body.

Finally when mergence of Ram and Sita takes place at the Apex center, Gangotri, the Ganga, the pure, cold and divine nectar/Amrit flows. That is only possible when soul as divine light merges with Supernal at the Apex center, consequently Gangotri -– the divine light and energy flow all around.

This is Real Ramayana and its inner meaning.

Chapter 9

Udana Prana, Mind, Breath and Divine Light

9.1 By generating the Udana Prana one can ascend Pranic energy up to Ajna chakra and beyond. Is it possible by merely observing breath and by its cessation there by, a spiritual aspirant/Sadhaka can reach up to Ajna chakra and beyond?

By Udana Prana/life force and its ascent through the spinal cord to reach the super conscious state is the Tantric method. This has been discussed in details:

By mentally observing the breath in and out i.e. by breath observation and later on gradually its cessation is the Gayatri concept. It is the approach to reach the super consciousness through breath cessation automatically for a few moments by wakeful awareness of breath. It gets ceased; stops automatically after some time; Sadhaka does nothing; only observes breath with concentration looking at the Ajna chakra by the eye-balls turned upwards. It is basically Shuniyaka method when no more fresh breath intake is there and inward breath has left the system. It is natural Shuniya – a void. It is the way of worship of spirit by awareness. Principally there is a difference of micro/nanosecond between the exhaust of inner breath and intake of the fresh breath. In this micro/nanosecond spiritual aspirant is without breath. It means he is apparently dead and with the cosmos – the Almighty spirit. If this interval is extended by the aspirant as if he takes breath by just merely counting as per his wishes, this will indicate that he is in awakening Turiya/transcendental state in the that interval; and he is with the spirit with full awareness. He is basically lively dead in such moments. This time gap is psychological time between the breaths and it is the time for the propagation of the spirit.

In this gap of breath in and out, the energy is created and exchanged. If the energy is not exchanged, it is the state of death. This worship/awareness of breath is known as SANDHYA; this is a Gayatri concept. The time gap without breath is ARAHA SANDHYA. It is like the gap between channels of two rails so that expansion of either rail can be absorbed in this gap. This gap between the subsequent breaths is basically energy center as the gap between two rails and energy from the cosmos gets absorbed in that interval and fresh abundance of energy goes in with the breath by the fresh intake. The more subtle pure energy is absorbed in the gap between the breaths as if more direct light enters the system and the Sadhaka remains in awakening Turiya state. It leads to Sushupati state with time and Sadhaka might enter in deep mental rest peaceful state gradually with more absorption of spiritual energy at the Ajna chakra. Parshurama has taught this technique. It is very effective and simple tool for self-absorption.

It is "PUNH PRANA PRANISHITA" way of worship. The divine light in Sadhaka attracts energy through nostril in this state. This is also termed as Pran Gayatri. The gap between breaths is Brahma. More the gap, the greater energy can get merged/absorbed with the intake coming breath.

This process is also termed as CHATURYAGA KARMA. This is Spanda/vibration of Gayatri. Exhaust of breath and not being intake is the "BRAHMO VEETA" state. This is also termed as Yagopaveeta and Gayatri Japa. This is not the outward Yagopaveeta. It is the highest inward Yagopaveeta. If one follows this way of Japa then he does not need wearing of outward Yagopaveeta and follow the external rituals of all kinds. This is the Sandhaya Vandhana by yogis without performing the external rituals at all. This is the supreme worship of Gayatri.

A Brahman needs to perform "UPANAYANA" – Sandhya Vandana three times a day.

The breath observation and attaining Shuniyaka/void inside is it self a Upanayana. No more Sandhaya is required if Sadhaka can attend this level of performing Sandhya by breath. Absence of breath with awareness is the real Gayatri Sandhya. On the other hand yogi performs Turiya Sandhya by breath control. This is Tantric Sandhya – A Tantric mode of Upasana.

As we know that eyes can detect the changes in picture on screen if the movement of picture is within certain minimum number of times. If the change in picture movement increases to more number of times, then eyes cannot detect. Similarly Shuniyaka can be observed if breath intake and exhaust is within some frequency. If this frequency is further reduced then the awareness ceases to exist and time between breaths intake and exhaust, being a long gap cannot be observed. Sadhaka becomes unaware of breath and then he is more time with spirit and thus he can reach to Turiya – Turiya state at the Ajna chakra and then the automatic conversion of Prana to light takes place that ascends automatically to Apex center without awareness and merges with the Supernal. Even at the Ajna chakra, intuition of Sadhaka increases. This increase of gap between the breaths in and breath out gives wonderful effects. This is basically spiritual way of breathing – a Gayatri mode. This spiritual practice/sadhana turns into Tantric Sandhya Upasana when awareness of breath changes to unawareness. It is then the stage of Samadhi in gradual steps. At this stage even if one is killed, he is totally unaware of this happening. This may happen when Udana Prana arrives little above to Ajna chakra i.e. to the Akula chakra.

From this level onwards one reaches from the known to the unknown zone and then from unknown to deep unknown zone. One can experience the primitive mystery of the cosmos. However one cannot describe this. This is AMANO state that is beyond word and mind. Neither word and nor mind can describe this state.

This is the science of soul. At this state the breath stops/gets suspended, and Udana Prana is gradually transformed into divine light. This experience cannot be described as the coitus experience of the couple during the climax of romance because this is beyond words, which both of partners experience during a few seconds of mergence/climax. Same way these mysteries of experience cannot be described.This all happens in psychosomatic plane. This cannot be explained since it is beyond concepts. It is action less action. This can be described by philosophy since it is an abstract experience. Abstract can be dealt with philosophy only. Merely relative experiences can be explained and discussed on the horizontal wordly plane. This abstract experience is visualized after cessation of complete breath. Only then one becomes totally inactive, and steps in the state of Shuniya/void. At this state there is no mind, no thought, no awareness, and such experiences are beyond apprehension. The increase of gap between breaths finally takes to such a high level and turns the physical body in to the spirit and divine light; and then there is nothing beyond this. It is the state of Savikalpa Samadhi that is beyond any description and apprehension.

9.2 Mind needs to be negated for ascending of Udana Prana/ life force but in horizontal plane mind must be full of awareness. This pendulum swinging of mind between unawareness required in ascending for vertical travel and full awareness needed for worldly activities creates misery to Sadhaka living in the horizontal plane. What then must he do? What is the remedy to deal with this critical situation?

This is a very practical problem for a spiritual aspirant/Sadhaka following the real divine path while engaged in the worldly activities living in the social environment. In general masses don't know about such problems. Only a few those who could make spiritual progress in the divine path of Self-realization have to face very critically such situations in the social dealings and in all worldly activities. Such people believe on others without understanding their selfish motives. On their face values and on their words they trust them and finally suffer to a major extent because the worldly people do not believe in ethics and values of dealings, and their own words. Finally worldly people easily and very frequently can deceive a divine person and they have to suffer miserably both inwardly and outwardly. Consequently spiritual persons blame themselves and their fate and take all miseries as their Prarabdha. This happens because they act without awareness as if mind is ceased to be there for worldly affairs, and is transcended most of the time and is merged in soul for upward journey toward Supernal. They act without using their mind fully while dealing with the worldly people; and act without complete awareness on the horizontal plane as if they are on the skyward journey. On the contrary, worldly people dealing with the horizontal plane activities don't believe any body unless they completely verify every minute details what the other party is saying. Still, even if they are trapped they have full capacity to fight and win over the opponents because of the fact that all such people belong to the same category and aware of all tactics. Where as spiritual personality suffers within him self very miserably since spiritual path does not allow him to fight unduly. He wants to win the self and his own committed mistakes by his silence, compassion and patience assuming all this is happening as per the God's wish.

A spiritual person sometimes lives in agony even to handle his own miseries. Being spiritual and his cutivated calmness do not allow him to react. His mind acts bilaterally. His mind starts fighting with his own mind. He loses the inbuilt mental calmness that he has cultivated by long spiritual efforts. Nobody is there to help him. His own mind plays dual game with him when he remembers all the episode/happenings. He blames himself; and thinks why he acted like this? He criticizes himself as if he is the biggest fool on the earth. He thinks in duality that he could have acted otherwise. He some times blames himself being spiritual that had made him weak by not even reacting on such critical situations. I ness; it ness; my ness; all stand against him to justify his mistakes. He admits mentally his mistakes but at the same time consider all this as the God's wish; since he feels otherwise it could have happened even worst; if he would have acted in different way before giving the said commitment. However, his subtle ego reminds him again and again through his subconscious mind and gets him mental agony. This is because of the fact that it is being taken up as bilateral stand by his mind alone. He tries to suppress the subtle ego mentally but remembers again and again and goes on suffering inside pretending to be silent inside. On the other hand the worldly person suffers only once by his blunted ego where as spiritual person suffer frequently till its effect is subsided.

The subtle ego breeds in spiritually. A divine person gets disturbed emotionally, psychologically and finally physically at times. His breath pattern gets disturbed; his blood circulation gets disturbed with time if the disturbances are not subsided. His normal spiritual activities get topsy – turvy. His sub-consciousness is the worst part of this bleeding ground. He may fall physically and mentally sick with this agony of stress since he cannot blame any body except himself. His own mind acts as the separate pole for himself. His mind thinks in duality. He suffers as he remembers. On the contrary, worldly person's mind under these conditions acts entirely on single pole and he acts firmly with the decisions he has taken. No duality of any kind exists in his thoughts. The spiritual person consciously acts with positive attitudes but his sub conscious mind acts with negative attitudes. There is severe conflict between sub conscious and conscious mind. His emotions and intellect have severe conflict beyond recognition within his own mind; and his harmony of the mind gets completely disturbed. His inner mental agony cannot be described by the words. However, outworldly he may able to maintain trans-quality.

Under such conditions of agony prevailing in the mind, the following spiritual techniques may help him. But the help will be temporarily only. These techniques temporary break the connection of conscious mind from the sub conscious mind; memories of the past will get subsided from the mind; but with lapse of time again the old memories will put their shadows on the mind and again suffering continues. Any way there is no other remedial measures except to follow the given techniques:

—Shunayaka /Void Method

This technique teaches to create void in the system by forcefully vacating the complete breath from the lungs/stomach etc. This leads to increase more of fresh energy inside that dilutes the effect of the memories of the sub conscious mind.

—Long inhalation and Exalation of Breath

This technique creates Shunayaka in the lungs and vitalizes the complete system with fresh divine energy of the breath. This also helps to break the linkage of sub conscious mind with conscious mind.

—To Remove Instantaneously Stored Breath in Head

This is the part of Kriya yoga, which gives strength to mind by removing the blocked impure air from head and rejuvenate the nerves of the head with fresh energy.

—Bringing the Eye Brows Closer by Closing Eyes

By this technique, the stored thoughts disappear from the mind by the pressure at the Ajna chakra when the eyebrows are brought closer by force with the closed eyes.

All the above techniques help to establish calmness and trans-quality temporarily with time by repeating as and when required. With these techniques the thoughts of sub conscious mind get subsided and mind gradually become more spiritual and strong, and takes all the agony with calmness without irritation.

The spiritual aspirant when in trouble must psychologically try to enjoy agony considering this as the minimum agony that the Almighty has bestowed on him being compassionate on him to uplift him and teach him a lesson to be careful in future.

All the above suffering is because of the X factor by the Almighty. This is probably the prarabdha and could not be avoided. There is no permanent remedy except to take it with patience showing the gratitude towards Almighty. Probably that is the reason why the spiritual man just agrees without much thinking by mind and giving any thought to the various issues. May be Maya, the Brahma, has withdrawn intellect and mind at that instance to make the one to suffer to refine him; to teach him more in due course.

Basically thought of past disturbs through memory to the spiritual person when he is in misery. He at times thinks about the reason and tries to justify and the conflicts starts in the mental level. All reactions and actions get stuck in his mind as duality, and the conflicts continue in the mind. Spiritual mind wants to find God with the presence of body. However, it is just not feasible. Since so far body is there, breath exists. In presence of breath, the spirit cannot prevail. So, all decisions taken by a spiritual person being in a physical form, whether he is aware or not aware of cannot be always correct. Because the decision is taken being in Maya i.e. in presence of breath, being in the physical form. These may be right or wrong depending on breath pattern. If a spiritual person takes crucial decision in Samadhi state, when breath is ceased, the decision cannot create any misery in life. Any crucial decision needs to be taken with intuition and not on the mental plane with logics, desires and attachments. Such decisions will be fatal and may prove to be wrong in due course if taken on the mental plane without intuition. This is because Srishti/world is imperfect. Human life is itself imperfect. Only a few seconds in Samadhi, when no role is played by mind and awareness, are the real useful moments of life. Any crucial decisions of life should be taken only after such a state of Samadhi to avoid miseries of future. Otherwise re-incumbent of memory will disturb with the thoughts if incorrect decisions that have been taken. If decision by conscious efforts, intentionally or with emotions are taken in the NIRAHA STATE –

in a state of Vairagaya/non-attachment, then only the decision will be selfless and correct. Briefly highlighting, the decision must be taken in the state of MANAH SANYASA, NIR MOHATA and CHID VIBHAVA state, then only it will be the right decision of life otherwise it might be trouble some and painful throughout the life.

In short mind cannot negate the negative capabilities is totality.

With mind there cannot be always all positive thoughts since the food of the mind is breath. The birth itself is a symbol of imperfection in all individuals since without breath the birth is not a reality. Death is a suspension of birth – the breath; and it is the only liberation – the cessation of breath. We all live in Maya and all our decisions are taken in Maya. Moreover Maya is a part of Brahma. So one must worship Maya and by propitiating Maya, we can take right decision since in Samadhi there is no mind, no thinking and there cannot be any wrong decision.

So the correct decision one can take in this world is by worshiping Maya, by the Maya and not being out of Maya. All decisions must be taken considering Maya/illusion, since every thing is in transit, and it should not create misery in one's mind. Furthermore, Maya is Jagdishwari.and awareness is the manifestation of Maya; all worldly/material related decisions must be taken in full consciouness/awareness only. Decision taken with unawareness even by a divine spiritual person will be fatal since we are 99 % in Maya in horizontal worldly plane and only 1% in the soul. To make correct decision in 1% state in the soul during decision-making is not practically feasible; so decision must not be taken in unaware stage. In addition Maya is Bhagwat Villas. And mostly every thing is the wish of Maya. Also, Aham in individual is Maya. Sada Shiva with the help of Maya has created cosmos so all worldly decisions are taken in Maya. Without the influence of Maya decisions cannot be taken. So Decisions must be taken with full awareness in all respects to avoid further misery. But once taken even wrong decision, even in Maya, prayers in Kutastha Chaitanya and manifestation of spirituality has full capability to rectify the wrong decision and correct them by the wish of Almighty since Maya is the part of Almighty. But one has to suffer till the effect of Maya is rectified by the grace of Almighty.

In nutshell, a divine person must bear all sufferings taking as God's will; and consider that the sufferings have come to give him to enrich him with more inside refinement; to uplift him and enlightened him. Basically the Almighty is the Karta/doer whether one does with awareness or without awareness. Both awareness and non-awareness are the two different poles of the same known and unknown energies. Every activity happens by His wish only. This is the real aspect and prospective of Self-realization that is beyond awareness and non-awareness.

Finally, as spiritual aspirant/Sadhak progresses in the upward spiritual path, vairagaya/dispassion is gradually developed in his mind. It is further manifested as he progresses in the spiritual path with time; he develops the capability to ride over the worldly miseries and overcomes all the suffering by the cultivated dissipation in his attitude to face the worldly people. Maya/illusion does not disturb him when vairagaya/dispassion rules the mental kingdom. Finally, for him all worldly issues/problems lose meaning and he conquers all his sufferings without any feel. He starts living face to face with the reality.

9.3 As the Udana Prana ascends and transforms into divine light at the Ajna chakra and goes up to Sahasrara, then the question arises is it possible that the divine light from the cosmos after descending through Apex center downward, couples with the Udana Prana/life force existing in the body?

This is very advanced question of spiritual science and to reply to this question only a Self-realized devotee/soul can give based on his experience/Anubhuti.

Prior to answering this question one must know that the Prana from the breath is extracted and it gets transformed to Vyana, Samana, and Apana. These four Pranas take up the complete activity of physical body and to keep proper function of the body. All auto system of the body covering transportation, distribution of energy, excrete system operation, breathing and so on are taken care of by Vyana, Samana, Apana and Prana, respectively. The Udana Prana needs to be generated at the Svadhisthanam by the spiritual practices and the close interaction of these four Pranas. Only the Udana Prana, thus generated, is transformed into life force and helps for spiritual development. Without Udana Prana, spiritual understanding and its enhancement/progress are not possible. It is the heart of spirituality and spiritual development. The gradual appearance of Udana Prana can be felt by the practices of Kriya yoga and it can be taken up through the Sushumna Nadi from Muladhara to Ajna chakra. Passing through Dhahara, it gives Nada and on crossing Visuddhi chakra and Lambika chakra, it becomes pure and concentrates at Kutastha Chaitanya. Here gradually passing through dream and Sushupati states, Udana Prana turns into pure light and ascends through Chidakasha towards Sahasrara and on the further ascend of divine light, it may merge with Supernal by the will of the Almighty. From this level, it can descend back to Ajna chakra and return to Muladhara. If this journey of life force and light continue for decades, this ascend and descend of light/ life force become Sahaja and thus spiritual aspirant can attained Savikalpa Samadhi.

Now, at times when spiritual aspirant/Sadhaka after years of spiritual practice looks within with the Sahaj Bhava and concentrates at the Apex center and Sahasrara chakra, he experiences the presence of divine light in the Chida akasha. If he is with this light exclusively for some times by the divine grace, he experiences or may experience that divine light from the cosmos penetrating through Apex center and spreads in the Sahasara. If this continues for a few moments and Sadhaka's eyeballs turn upwards, this light may descent downward through Unmani chakra by its own and gradually gets settled in Ajna chakra. Since the pathless path exists in Chida Akasha for ascend and descend of light, this descend by its own does not create any resistance. It looks as if divine Amrit/nector is pouring from Chida akasha to the Ajna chakra.

Under the above conditions, Sadhaka is in automatic meditation without any self-efforts. The respiratory system of Sadhaka works with usual slow breathing. This is the phenomenon occurring beyond Ajna chakra i.e. in between Ajna chakra and Sahasrara. This is the state of awakening —— Turiya i.e. awakening transcend state. The Sadhaka can step into Turiya —— Turiya state if he just desires and wishes since he is with the divine light in the Chida akasha. It is the blissful state. To be just like this for the time being one can pray and recite Mantra as per his wish, based on his status and initiation. To be with this light in Chida akasha is a timeless state and when Sadhaka is back to the awakening consciousness then only he finds the time that has passed. In this state breath is tranquil and breathing is continued from both the nostrils. Basically this light in the Chida Akasha is the combination of Pranic energy in the form of kinetic energy and the converted divine light from cosmos. Through hairs in the skull this cosmic light flows and comes in contact with kinetic Pranic energy ascending from Ajna chakra; and when this link is established then kinetic Pranic energy and divine cosmic light get enhanced in the Apex center, Sahasrara and Chidakasha. After some time this Pranic kinetic energy and cosmic light descend to the Ajna chakra; gradually this net energy transformed as life force get concentrated at Ajna Chakra. Furthermore, by the wish and desire of Sadhaka/spiritual aspirant life force can descend from Ajna/Lambika to Visuddhi to Dhahara, Manipura, Swadhisthanam to Muladhara; on this location again spiritual aspirant feels the sensation of Prana as earlier, which is nothing but the presence of life force /Udana Prana on its backward journey from Apex centre; this Prana/ energy can again ascend to Apex center by the yoga Sadhana of the Sadhaka in a Sahaj/easy way by the grace of the Almighty; and thus its forward and backward travel continues.

In short the answer of this query is very simple and can be put in simple words that divine light after re-transformation can travel back to Muladhara by itself provided Sadhaka has followed the ascend path for decades and this pathless path has already been established. Then only without generating Udana Prana in the system and just by the grace of Almighty the divine cosmic energy can be poured to Apex center; and through Sahasrara to Ajna it can travel as divine light; and gradually it transform as Pranic life force and is converted back to Udana Prana. Thus this all is possible but not by the beginners but by advanced Sadhakas and only by the grace of Almighty and Cosmic Mother and as per their wish only.

9.4 Why suddenly the mind of spiritual aspirant/ Sadhaka gets disturbed? Is it because of extra sensitive perception of his mind?

The mind of a Sadhaka is a very sensitive antenna, more sensitive than an ordinary person. Any inner and external disturbances because of his close association and attachment, with his closest associates, can give the exact signals of their problems that can disturb his mind being highly sensitive, fragile and pure. This is a basically the sense of oneness of the Sadhaka with his associates and particularly with his kith and kin. It is a natural and the mysterious phenomenon. Sometimes even the shock is felt when undue happening occurs. It is unavoidable because of the linkage of fate with the happenings. It is in fact a Prarabdha that is even beyond the best possible efforts of an individual to avoid them. Under these conditions a Sadhaka cannot do any thing; he can just pray Almighty and prepare himself for the undue gimmicks/ happenings of the fate. His breath becomes restless; but by self-control and bringing back the tranquil breath, the Sadhaka/spiritual aspirant temporarily can come out of the miseries of the shock waves striking his mind. Although the troubles continue for the Sadhaka until the conditions become normal but that takes its own time. Beyond that nothing can be done since all these are closely linked with the psychological attachment. All these disturbing thoughts, because of highly psychological linkage of the Sadhaka with his associates, get stored in the sub conscious mind. At time when these disturbing thoughts are surfaced on the conscious mind, the mental peace of the Sadhaka is disturbed. All this is closely linked with the negative memories of the sub consciousness. These are beyond the control of even advanced Sadhaka to nullify their effects. However, temporarily by Shuniyaka process, breathe control and re-establishment of the tranquil breath, the mental peace can be restored by intensive efforts that break the close ties of the conscious mind with that of the sub conscious mind temporarily.

Conscious mind is always filled with the energy but not with the memories. The memories of sub conscious mind surfaced on the conscious mind having abundance of kinetic energy get involved easily with the thought process of the memories. This disturbs the self-control that leads to loss his peace of mind; and makes him violent at time if accompanied with the disturbed pattern of breath. Even 2/3 of the higher mind can get disturbed because of the suffocation of tranquil breath by the lack of oxygen supplied by the horizontal/physical breath. Even subjective fear disturbs the tranquil breath. Memories of the past events stored in the emotional heart swallow the tranquil breath. This happens some times even without the touch and participation of the mind. It is automatic disturbance if exceeds the limits of emotions in the heart. Tranquil breath is regenerated as the storm of acute disturbance is subsided, however, it may take long time to get the harmony re-established in the system. The re-appearance of tranquil breath is indirectly proportional to the strength of mind. It means that if the mind is stronger then tranquil breath can be established fast. On the contrary if reactions of the various actions in mind are more severe, the mind become weak and it takes long duration for establishment of tranquil breath. This is the situation of psychological malady for an individual. One can be persecuted even because of this malady. He suffers like a most ordinary person out of miserable fear and different types of disturbing doubts in his mind. Consequently, it takes longer time to re-establish the tranquil breath that gives him peace.

In every body's life both good and bad happens and one must be prepared for the worst. Only ego of a person does not want to compromise on any front. Spiritual person is supersensitive and he suffers more on any front. It is because of the fact that he brings himself above Maya, and Maya – the greatest force cannot tolerate this and always put him in problems/miseries one after the other. Above Maya means as if on the top branch of a tree and this is likely to have much less stiffness and with a slight blow of wind, it can easily shake. It is the case with the highly evolved spiritual person that he has to suffer much more than a common man. It is the way of life for him being a supersensitive. A common man lives on horizontal plane totally merged in Maya and so Maya do not create much suffering for him. Also, he becomes more insensitive because of the effect of Maya/illusion and just does not get disturbed unless the major issue comes on his way. In general every body suffers in life, on what so ever plane he is. One cannot completely choose his plans, life and ways/means. The invisible force does most of the things for him. Only precaution for the spiritually evolve person is that he must refuse to react under any circumstances. He must maintain silence since it is both gold and God. Only if he reacts he has to suffer more internally than a common human being. Spiritual person must always try to keep his sub-conscious as clear and as right as possible so that stored thoughts must not get surfaced on conscious plane and disturb him. Sub conscious state can only be checked by tranquil breath. Negative thoughts on the conscious plane can be checked and controlled only by yoga Sadhana.

To disturb somebody, the only technique is to awaken the negative thoughts in his sub conscious state by the negative approach of the close associates who must disturb his tranquil breath. In the war of Mahabharata, Karana's tranquil breath was disturbed by ALIA – his charioteer – who always talked negative about Kauravas and praised Pandavas as per the instructions of Lord Krishna. This indirectly disturbed the tranquil breathe of Karana and disturbed/agitated his mind to such an extent so that he could take up the correct decision in the war in favour of Pandavas.

Human mind is always conscious and it can be peaceful under the effect of tranquil breath. Subconscious mind is always subjective and under the effect of X-factor, it can bring the subconscious past memories on the conscious mind and can disturb and deteriorate the tranquil breath irritating the peaceful mind. The suffering of a person cannot be fully eliminated till then the consciousness is there. In this world neither peace and nor war, and nothing else is permanent. Every thing is mutative. All human experiences are a passing phase only. Nothing remains permanent in the mind. Subjective conscious breath pattern due to its mutative thinking disturbs mind. It can be controlled only by tangible tranquil breath. One must resurrect tranquil breath as soon as possible if the reactions of conscious mind are very powerful. Conscious mind is full of emotional instincts. Basically human Mind is BHAVA and it is SANSARA. We are drowned in Maya. Mind needs to be kept in balance by tranquil breath to face the mental disturbances both from inside and out side. If the influence of spirit is more predominant, it will be faster to get established tranquil breath in him, but again his behavior is like an elephant who after taking bath puts all the mud on him self again. Exactly similar is the case with breath that swings between horizontal and tranquil breaths as mind swings between disturbance and peace. The evil spirits and negative thoughts always disturb tranquil breath. It is like a crab that wants to cross and go to the top of the vessel to get free but other crabs push him down. Similarly tranquil breath cannot be permanent and regularly is disturbed and put back with the horizontal breath like a crab crossing the boundary, who will again and again force fully is pushed back by the other crabs in the vessel.

Basically, conscious feeling of attachment cannot be erased and a man suffers again and again as the attachment will not allow the establishment of tranquil breath. It will be periodically disturbed by the subconscious feelings. The approach is to unburden the disturbed feelings and not to invite the memories from the subconscious state of the causes for these disturbed feelings on the conscious plane. To live in the present without being in touch with past and future is the best way to be away from these miseries. In other words be SAKSHI/Vigilant/Observer of the mental thoughts appearing in the mind, which will get subsided by its own. Finally this will lead to create thoughtless state and tranquility of the mind gets established. This is only possible by maintaining the tranquil breath as long as possible. Furthermore, Sadhaka must be introvert to be in the soul light to have the total mental peace. A common man can bear the load of disturbed feelings much easier being more insensitive than a spiritually evolved highly sensitive person can. He is easily reconciled being on a horizontal plane than an intellectual spiritually evolved person. Basic intellect and spiritual evolution make a person more sensitive, emotional and more concerned for others. He becomes helpless spectator of all the circumstances. He wants to follow the path of least resistance in the horizontal activities and tries to find conveniences so that he could direct his energy for vertical travel. But, a common man living in horizontal plane takes that what so ever is happening, is normal in every walk of life, since he is highly insensitive and can fight the issues and resolve them boldly by right or wrong means, and he does not need to conserve his energy to follow the vertical path.

So in short, a Sadhaka gets disturbed very easily for any problem of the horizontal plane but a common man takes every problem as the tide to ride and solve it without getting much disturbed. A Sadhaka needs energy for higher cause to take vertical path and for a common man no conservation of energy is needed for any other purposes than to be in horizontal plane and to deal the problems of this plane only. However, as Sadhaka progress in his spiritual journey, gradually vairagaya/dispassion develops in the core of his heart that makes him very strong in the worldly affairs and soon he raises much above that of the horizontal plane and the issues of this mundane world. He becomes contented and happy in all respects.

9.5 What precisely happens to life force/divine light after the Akula Chakras?

All the chakras below the Ajna charka are named as Kula Chakras. Only the chakras above Ajna chakra are called Akula chakra. There are total nine chakras above Ajna chakra including Unmani, Sahasrara, and Apex center and so on.

The Udana Prana ascends up to Ajna chakra through the Sushumna Nadi. Basically, after passing through Dhahara, Visuddhi, and Lambika, it must be a pure light at the Ajna Chakra. But, generally, it reaches at this junction mixed with Udana Prana with subjugation of Jeevatma, mind and Kundalini power. Gradually mind gets dissolved here in the soul and Jeeva is isolated, and soul as pure light after conversion of Udana Prana as light travels up through the Akula chakras, for mergence with the Supernal on crossing Chida akasha. Principally travel of light through Akula Chakras must be with non-awareness as the spiritual aspirant should be in Turiya/transcendence state after crossing Sushupati state. But, the ascendance even through Akula Chakras for most of the spiritual aspirants/ Sadhakas is mixed with Udana Prana and not as the pure divine light. It is partly with awareness and partly with unawareness. Even Prana keeps partially its separate identity and the Sadhaka most of the time is in awakening transcendence/ Jagrit Turiya state.

It means the Kundalini even in Akula Chakras is the Maya. Kundalini is not in its pure form even at the Akula Chakras. It shows that yoga, Tantra, Dyana/meditation have been performed with awareness. It may turn to unawareness/Laya state/Samadhi, or not, cannot be assured in totality. Even under this level of achievement, nectar of light from the cosmos pours through the Apex center and feeds the rising Kundalini at the Akula Chakras. Even if Kundalini has arisen up to the lower Chakras than the Ajna, nectar of light coming from an Apex center is absorbed by the Kundalini on these levels. If the flow of this light from Apex center is stopped by any reason, human being cannot live. This process of light, descend of light from Apex center to the Kundalini is automatic and it is continued without stoppage even to an ordinary person. This cosmic light makes us alive until it is not absorbed by the Kundalini. If the Kundalini arises three and half coil above the Apex center, this light is no more absorbed by the Kundalini and it gets released. This light then spreads in the Chida akasha and a Sadhaka is merged with cosmic light within him and he is inside the light. There is direct communication of cosmic light with the light in the Chida akasha. It is the stage of mergence/Laya and Samadhi.

As soon as the Kundalini descends down from the Apex center, the light starts getting absorbed by the Kundalini and light is not allowed to get dissipated on the lower organs including Linga. A human life thus continues. Rising of Kundalini is the spiritual evolution and as well getting debarred from Maya is the main purpose of life. Furthermore, on arising the Kundalini, divine light descending from the Apex center is absorbed directly by the Kundalini without much of its dissipation. Kundalini at the higher Chakras/Akula Chakras after ascendance from Muladhara absorbs direct divine light, and thus all the divine qualities are poured/ developed by much faster pace in the spiritual aspirant that leads for accelerated spiritual evolution in him. The effect of Maya: attachment; greediness; evil qualities; etc., gradually start diminishing from the built in character of the sadhaka. Thus, the awakening of Kundalini and direct absorption of divine light from the cosmos accelerate achievement of illumination with divine qualities.

Spirituality is the play of anti-poles i.e. Maya and the divine light. Maya is a part of Brahma. Evolution of Sadhaka in Maya to divinity and manifestation of divine light in him makes him Self-realized and divine personality in course of time.

The Udana Prana, when converted into light, gives energy to the brain cells, when Prana/light spreads in each and every cell of the brain and makes it healthy with the adequate supply of oxygen. Prana also supply energy to 72000 Nadis of the physical body, make it healthy and keep its functions without any problems. Even function of the body muscles is properly catered by the Pranic energy. Prana contains the subtle energy of all the five elements i.e. earth/food, water, fire/Agni, air, Akasha/ether and these are appropriately distributed by the different Pranas in the system. Prana also takes care of organic aspects of the system. It takes care of consciousness/Chetana and also carries soul light to Akula Chakras through Kundalini, and finally itself get transformed in to the divine light for further mergence with the Supernal.

Life force at the Ajna Chakra and onwards i.e. in the Akula chakra is the divine light. Breath is suspended in the Akula Chakras. Only a part of light contains Prana that gives slight awareness to Sadhaka in meditation in the Turiya state. But in the state of total mergence /Samadhi, there is no awareness otherwise Samadhi will not be real/Pooran Samadhi. If one has experienced mergence, he cannot describe it. It is beyond description in all respects. It is only feasible when in the Akula Chakra where Prana is totally transformed into the divine light. Mukhya/main Prana must be transformed in to divine light otherwise it will be a case that one has reached Ganga, but could not take bath. Kundalini, at this stage if not properly directed, may act as a dangerous snake. It must bliss the Sadhaka coming out from the Brahmarandhara center otherwise it may affect the various centers of the Akula Chakras.

To achieve the above, the Prana must contain only Akasha element and all other elements of the Udana Prana must be dropped before or at the Visuddhi chakra. Then only pure transformation of light can take place. Mind and Jeeva will be isolated and pure soul light will ascend in the Akula Chakra that leads to the state of Samadhi and mergence with the Supernal.

In short, beyond Akula chakra, Kundalini blesses the Sadhaka after taking out its snake hood above the apex center. In this stage, divine light spreads in the Chida akasha and breath is totally suspended; this leads sadhaka/spiritual aspirant to enter in the state of Samadhi without awareness; he is then blessed with all the divine qualities. Finally, his soul merges with the Supernal. He is then in Savikalpa/Nirvikalpa Samadhi.

Chapter 10

'AUM' Technique and Dhyana/ Meditation

10.1 What is the AUM technique? How this technique must be followed for Self- realization?

AUM is the most respectable, worship able, adorable word of Hindu religion and Indian mythology. Other religious sects use similar words as "AMEEN" "EK AUM KAR" etc with the same respect. From the core all these adorable words have the same sound AUM. This is only the sound that is produced without rubbing of two forms/surfaces in close interactions. It is produced by the flow of the air from the mouth through the system without causing any friction between two forms/surfaces on interaction.

AUM is pranava and it has 5 matras; it means that there are 5 stages of AUM recitation. If AUM is not chanted properly; there is no generation of bio spiritual energy in the system. Five matras of AUM are A, U, M, (moon/crescent), and (.) dot /bindu. The five stages of AUM recitation depicts that Nada by recitation of A i.e. AKARA, should merge into U i.e. Ukara and then into M i.e. MAKARA. After this at the Ajna chakra, a slight/mild feeling is experienced as if crescent; the half moon is lifted upwards. This pleasant mild pressurized feeling is due to the net Nada/sound produced by the AUM in between the eyebrows. This state and feeling at this junction is named as Turiya Sandhya. Beyond this location light must be felt as dot/bindu traveling upwards. This uplifts/raises the Sadhaka to the threshold of Turiya/transcendental state. This is known as SAVADA AUM. Under this state the feeling of sparkle of light of crescent in the forehead shall be clearly felt, which shows the correct practice of AUM by a Sadhaka. The AUM sound felt at the Ajna chakra is termed as NADA LINGA. It gets transformed into the divine light. At the Ajna chakra, the vibration of ARDH CHANRA facing upwards is essential; it to be felt to satisfy the correctness of chanting AUM and magnetization of biospiritual atoms of the system gradually.

The conscious of the Sadhaka at the Bhurugati junction (between the eye brows) turns upwards by NADA LINGA as a consequence of AUM recitation correctly. This is the point of third eye location. Beyond this point there is quiescence of AUM NADA i.e. no nada is produced beyond this point. It is the end of NADA at this location. This point is termed as NADA ANTA. At this point Sadhaka must feel natural Shuniya/void. Breath is suspended at this location. No feeling of Nada is experienced beyond this location/point; only the divine light appears with time. Every thing including mind, life force, Nada, jeeva must get dissolve at this location; and beyond this point only pure soul light, the divine light, that is beyond time, space and causation/consciousness exists. Basically life force/ Prana, Nada and consciousness become one, a single identity i.e. light; it happens beyond Ajna chakra/Bhurugati. The Prana becomes subtle along with light and follows the AVATAR NADA ANUSANDHANA.

The control of Prana by AUM chanting is through AUM KUMBIKA and RECHAKA that leads to the visiting of temple of light through AUM. "A" of AUM is termed as Srishti/world; "U" of AUM is Sidhiti/sustenance of the world/Srishti that is the mystery of cosmos; "M" of AUM is Pralaya/dissolution; Crescent/half moon is Tridhana where Nada, Udana Prana and Consciousness are merged; and dot/bindu is the light/Uamana that travels skyward to merge with the Supernal. AUM depicts DRIG, DRISHAYA and light as the cosmic mystery that the entire cosmos must merge in bindu/dot; and when it happens in the Chida akasha to the Sadhaka, it is nothing but Turiya/transcendental state. Turiya state is the threshold of Samadhi. It is a semi bliss state and it is possible to achieve by AUM technique.

Sadhaka crosses from SAVADA AUM to AVADHA AUM before reaching to PRORAJAS at Sahasrara chakra. At this stage it is without BHAVA and beyond seeing, seen and seer etc. It is oneness state i.e. the mergence state. No more consciousness is left at this state. No energy, no ascendance at Sahasrara and the residual energy are felt to spread as light in Chida akasha. This light illuminates Chida akasha at the Sahasrara and no ascend of light takes place beyond this by AUM technique.

Principally AUM is NADA ROCKET that carries Prana along with Nada. Nada controls Prana and leads to unconscious Shuniyaka state by correct chanting of AUM. It is not forced and intentional void/Shuniyaka; it is just natural unconscious void/Shuniyaka by chanting of holy mantra AUM. Upto Ajna chakra, Sadhaka feels Prana, Nada and Consciousness but beyond that it is atomic energy of Prana that gets converted into light and spreads as illumination of enlightenment in the Chida akasha; and Sadhaka tends to be self realized in due course.

No mantra is equivalent to AUM that leads to give Self-realization by just its correctly chanting with devotion. It emits 10 types of Nada by correct chanting at the Ajna Chakra and finally merges as divine light.

It is the wonder of AUM technique and highest blessing to mankind by the Almighty.

10.2 What is Dyana/meditation and preparation needed on physical and mental planes to commence it? Where meditation does finally leads?

What is Dyana/Meditation? It is very complex to explain. This is because in meditation, one is not there then how it can be explained what it is? One is totally merged in meditation in self and then he becomes totally unaware. If one is aware it means he is not in Dyana. Then he is a separate identity, observing the happenings within and without, he is merely a spectator and not in meditation. Under such conditions one is not within it. And if one is within it then only he loses his identity. Conscious meditation/ Jagrik Turiya/awakening transcendental state is not the ultimate of meditation. What any body talks or try to define is only the conscious state and Dyana/meditation with awareness. It is the starting junction of meditation and most of us end meditation at this junction only even after life long practice. One gets only marginal benefit out of such meditation. So even for this what preparations are needed shall be discussed. First and foremost is Dyana Bumika/preface of meditation; one needs to learn this from a self realized Guru. One needs to concentrate on Triputi junction i.e. the point between eyebrows; and even for this some basic preparations are required to concentrate.

The followings are the basic prerequisites before starting the meditation:

1. On the physical plane, the body must be healthy. Stomach must be empty. It means the best time for meditation is morning and evening hours. But at least there must be 4-5 hours gaps between the food intake and the meditation.

2. Inner system of the Dhyani/meditator must be healthy in all respects. Before starting meditation some breathing exercises must be done to feel fully relaxed. These can be forceful breathing exercises basically using Shuniyaka technique, Kriya yoga and so on; so that Udana Prana is well generated in the system.

3. All past thoughts from the mind must be removed. One must learn to live in present. What is "now", it is every thing.

Consider that past is dead and future is uncertain/unwritten. No fear for future to be kept in mind. Consider you are the lord of present. Since one can use only present and can command it as he wishes? No need to brood on past. Projection of past only creates confusion and most of us waste our life to be living and thinking of past only. One must attend/check even smallest appearance of thoughts in the present before meditation so that it should not manifest in due course.

4. The place of sitting for meditation must be comfortable. Meditator must face east, or west or north. Outer noise must be the minimum around the sitting space and circulation of fresh air shall be adequate. It is better if plants, green curtains are around and environment is natural. Seashore, bank of the river, water tank and plants/trees around give much inspiration to the Meditator and add to his inner peace.
5. Meditation is a psychosomatic exercise so the inner peace, outer calmness and peaceful environment help to evolve the Meditator.
6. The best preparation for meditation is equivalent to the 2/3 of the achievement. After well preparation, Meditator must chant the Mantra given by the Satguru and be attentive at the Triputi/ in between the eyebrows. This is gross awareness stage. Later Meditator must close eyes, remember his Guru, Ishtdevata and switch on from gross Mantra recitation to the Mona/silent Japa. This gradually brings the gross stage to the subtle stage to the Meditator with the conscious awareness. This is the second Bhumika for the meditation.
7. In third Bhumika, Meditator must start Kriya yoga without chanting the Mantra. This gives rise to awareness of Prana in the system. This yoga paditi/system is known as Raj yoga. If the Prana is evolved, the progress in yoga becomes very fast. On the contrary if there occurs mal functioning of various Pranas in the system, different stomach problems start originating and success in yoga/ meditation becomes difficult. The Meditator must take immense care for correct/adequate distribution of various Pranas in the system by breathing exercises and self-management.

8. Human body is microcosm and cosmos is macrocosm. The Udana Prana/life force is generated in the microcosm; on traveling through Sushumna Nadi of the spinal cord passing through different charkas, it reaches to Ajna chakra; and then to Chida akasha; and gradually getting transformed into light, which merges with the Supernal. When Udana Prana reaches trinity, awareness of breath diminishes and gradually awareness of Prana is loosened. This state is known as CHATUR YAGA KAMMA. This happens in gradual steps from awakening to dream state to DRUG/SUSHUPATI state. In this state Meditator is not aware of breath and not of Mantra recitation. It is half conscious mixed Bhumika state. Also, Jeeva is released from the soul gradually; if Jeevatma ascends to this level along with or in place of pure soul. It is half or semi mergence state just above the Tirupati. Half of the awakening consciousness is lost at this level. Further to this NISHKARIYA BOOMIKA state is reached when Jeeva/living being's conscious awareness merges into soul completely. No more minds' existence is left here; it is the functionless state. Life force/ Prana merges with soul and Meditator starts getting cosmic consciousness and his third eye is gradually opened after years of such practice by the grace of Almighty.

9. Meditator is still conscious. His conscious is not yet released. This happens at the Ajna chakra. This is the Kutakash Chaitnaya state. After this stage transformation of light occurs from Udana Prana. With the appearance of light and its ascendance to Chida Akasha there is no more time, space consciousness. It is the state of universal oneness. Meditator starts considering all human being are alike and he inherently develops state of universal brother hood by its own. He develops divine qualities/virtues of forgiveness, love, renunciation, no hatred, humility, truthfulness and like these 27 quartiles are developed as described by Lord Krishna in Gita for a divine spiritual aspirant; as He Himself being perfect in all these qualities. This is the conscious Turiya/ transcendental state. It is the state of monistic dualism but not the state of mergence in the sky.

10. As the light further ascends to the Chida akasha. It crosses the state of TIRUPATI BHANGA, where there is; no time; no space; and no consciousness; concept. All the three identities time, space and consciousness become one. As this pure light further ascends, it reaches UNMANI, where it spreads and awareness is lost. This is VIDHEHA STATE of evolution.
11. Finally when it reaches Sahasara, it becomes center of source light. Meditator enters in the state of Samadhi at Sahasara. And to the Apex center when this ascends, it blesses to the Meditator the glimpses of Para Samadhi. Moment this divine light merges with the macro cosmos, spiritual aspirant is in the state of Nirvikalpa Samadhi; and as this light returns back to Ajna and subsequently to Muladhara chakra, it gives the blessings and experience of Svikalpa Samadhi to the Meditator/ Dhayani. Thus with this Meditator achieves "nothing" but every thing.

The above explains preparation for meditation, meditation technique and the final

Achievement of the meditation.

10.3 What is Sandhya in general and what happens during the Sandhya period i.e. time interval between breath exhalation and inhalation?

Evolution starts from Bindu/point. The static energy of Bindu is partially gets converted into the kinetic energy during evolution. Thus, the manifestation continues from the un-manifested static Bindu/point since cosmic energy is in seed form in the Bindu that is in the un-manifested static stateless state. By the unknown reasons, Spandau in the Bindu leads to various kinds of intensive throbbing in the Bindu, and part of the Bindu that was static, un-manifested, the manifestation commences in it. Thus in the dualist pattern of the Bindu, consisting of manifested and un-manifested parts, out of which the un-manifested part gets manifested and turns into many-ness. Thus the creativity by throbbing comes out of dielectric in the series one after the other and multiplying pattern is continued.

The Spandau creates close interaction in the Bindu that leads to throbbing, which generates mysterious force that multiplies within the Bindu and manifestation is continued. This is the origin of the Cosmos from Bindu by Spandau and throbbing. With out Spandau there cannot be creation and no creativity is feasible. Cosmic Spandau is because of the desire of Almighty. The linkage between various states of the Bindu is through the Spandau and it is not the continued process. Between manifest state/Sada Shiva/ Shiva/Kameshwara and Shakti, and the un-manifested state, there is gap – the Kala – the time – the awareness, which always exists. Thus the triangle is formed with time, manifested and un-manifested states. Without time no transformation takes place. So, Spandau is Kala – the time. The cosmic throbbing is nothing but time, space and consciousness, which generate the other-ness and thus the Bindu/point, continues the multiplication. The initially – un-manifested – Bindu, the Ishwara, were existed. By His desires; manifestation; Kameshwara; awareness appeared and under the effect of Spandau – the Kala – time, the manifestation in many-ness continued. Kala is the division of absolute, wholeness, one-ness into many-ness. Desire of absolute is Kama Kala; it is the Maha Maya that created the otherness. Mother of otherness is Kal Mahimani, Nara Hamasi, Lalita, Chandi and so on. The initial state of un-manifested i.e. AKAL MANIMANI is changed partially to MAHA MAYA, which is Kali, by the Spandau. Spandau is cosmic dance by Kala/time rhythm that creates manifestation from un-manifested Bindu.

Absolute, the God measures everything in time frame where as measurement by man is in the material/the Anu form that is the relative knowledge. Time is the evolution, however in the material plane, it is governed by atom. But time creates material/atom in the absolute terms under the influence of natural conditions.

There are four Sandhyas in a day. They are Udaya Sandhya (morning by 6 a.m.), Madhya Sandhya (12 noon), Swaimi Sandhya (by 6 p.m.) and the Turiya Sandhya at 12'O clock midnight.

Basically, the gap, when other-ness is likely to approach from the existing state is called Sandhya. This other-ness is Maya. As night darkness changes to daylight, the time gap for the dawn is Sandhya. The change to other-ness from the original state is Sandhya. Similarly, as the earth position with respect to sun changes, the changes of seasons occur. There are 12 seasons in year with change of 30-degree position of the earth. That completes one complete cycle in 12 months. In the same way consciousness (Chaitanya) has four Sandhyas i.e. Jagrik to Swapna to Sushupati to Turiya and then to Turiya Tita (the mergence).

In the same way mind has four Sandhya i.e. mind to Buddhi (intellect) to Chita(consciousness) to Ahankara (ego). The transit gap between thinking and execution of activities by different sections of the mind is Sandhya. The whole world is full of Spandau (gaps) between the two different states. Between life and death, there is a gap; the Spandau; and thus both are the "other-ness" for each other. This Spandau, the gap, is called the light. In other words this light is time since with time it becomes other-ness and changes. The time that leads to changes is nothing but the cause of evolution. Thus the Spandau that leads to throbbing is the change of evolution and mother of creativity. Every thing of the manifestation is governed by time and also the un-manifested to the manifested state revolves around time. Time leads to other-ness; it is Spandau; and when a one-ness change to other-ness is called Sandhya.

Catching of Sandhya; the time gap of the changes; is the creativity. So creativity is the change of pattern under the influence of Spandau, and it is governed by time. Creativity is the mother of all inventions. Basically, it is in the entrance of void; the gap; and the time; when the change of states is taking place. The Sandhya is worshiping able Gayatri. It is the direct link with the infinity. It is the light, which transforms the other-ness with time. The contemplation on this light gives all creative ideas related to the deep secrets of the cosmos, which can be manifested and can make wonderful discoveries. Newton and Einstein could probe into Sandhya and could catch the essence of creative light for the various discoveries of this nature. The triangle of life and death is completed by the appearance of silence; the Spandau; the gap; the time; and that is the secret of cosmos.

The individual consciousness to the cosmic consciousness is the Sandhaya that links the soul to the Paramatma/Almighty. This Spandau; the function variation; from relative to the Absolute and vice versa from Absolute to relative is the Sandhya that completes the triangle of soul and Paramatma; it gives the mystery of Self-realization and mergence of soul with the Supernal. To be aware of this Sandhya; this time gap; reveals the mystery of every thing but this comes by His grace only.

Sandhya links two infinite versions of life and death; also it links soul and Paramatma. To be in other-ness from one-ness through awareness in Sandhya; it is the mystery of the mysteries. From awareness stage to non-awareness stage of Samadhi is the Sandhya. From microcosm to macrocosm is through Sandhya. From awareness of time to the state of timeless-ness is through Sandhya. The Sandhya completes the triangle to other-ness; and to be with it, is the secret of all the creativities of the Almighty. One has to enter into this gap and who enters is the conqueror of the universal/ cosmic secrets. The state of Samadhi is the mergence of soul with the Supernal through the Sandhya of timeless-ness i.e. shading of awareness. Without Spandau- the time gap, there is no Sandhya. Shiva is the creator of this Spandau, Shakti is the throbbing and time is the energy. So by interaction of Shiva and Shakti in the Sandhya of time, energy is evolved. It means energy is created through time. In other words energy; the light; is the time. In more subtle form time can create Anu/molecule and Pramanu/atom. Thus time is light. Light/energy creates matter and vice versa matter can create energy. So, energy is Sandhya from the infinity. From time, all types of knowledge is created; it is Paramajyothi. It is Lalita, Parameshwari. Para Gayatri is Absolute; and Apara Gayatri is matter.

In short, time is the faith of God and it is Spandau; Sandhya; light; energy; and transformation to different matters. And this is the mystery of mysteries of cosmos, which can be perceived through Sandhya only.

10.4 Out of the various techniques of Dyana/meditation i.e. Udana Prana technique, AUM technique and Sandhya Gayatri technique, which technique should be followed. Or, Sadhaka/spiritual aspirant can follow any technique depending on his system needs and his own mental and physical throbbing/vibrations.

All the techniques of Dyana/meditation are the perfect techniques. One must perfect one of the techniques and follow it regularly; he will succeed to the path of Self-realization. All the techniques lead to mergence. In meditation there is no mind and not even divisible mind; no time concept; and no awareness, which lead to the oneness with the cosmos. No disintegrate and separateness – total oneness with the cosmic awareness to become one with that supreme is the final achievement by following one of these techniques.

Ahankara; Chitta/ consciousness to become integral is the basic and foremost requirement. Particularly, Ahankara is the motivation and decision-making faculty, and Chita/consciousness is the logical base; and these are the pro and cons of the decision-making faculty. One has mind, buddhi (intellect), Chitta (consciousness) and Ahankara before action is undertaken and even after the action has been executed. After action there can be reaction in mind and intellect. Chitta – the consciousness can manifest the reaction. Ahankara is the manifested consciousness; and may be divisible or integrated consciousness; it depends on the reaction of mind and intellect after the action.

All the above four constituents give the various capabilities to a human being. Mind revolves around the Ichha Shakti. It revolves around the desires; their creation; ways and means; so as to fulfill all of them. Budhi/intellect and Chitta/conscious revolve around Gyana/knowledge. With accumulation of knowledge, help/ assistance is rendered to accomplish desires created by mind; where as Ahankara/egoism is the Kriya; the final action taken to execute the activity to fulfill desires. Without Aham/ego- self-activity cannot be undertaken. Although activity has been desired, knowledge is gathered but without the force of Aham/ego –self — the Jeeva, it cannot be put into action to accomplish. Furthermore, it must be understood that mind is atomic in nature, and. it is very subtle and mutative. The silence cannot enter into the mind easily unless mind become greatest and enter into super conscious state. The moment it enters in the super conscious state, awareness goes; no more existence of mind remains; and only silence prevails. So when there is silence; there is no mind; no awareness. It is stateless state of super conscious but without consciousness and awareness. It is intuitive state; divine state of Svikalpa Samadhi since one cannot be there for a long duration. This state may come and go. How it comes and goes, it is only the play of Almighty. In this state physical microcosm merges into macrocosm of the cosmos. This integrity is the stateless state of Samadhi; if prolonged, it becomes non-return state to the awareness; it is then called Nirvikalpa Samadhi.

Sandhya Gayatri is the technique, which leads to take Sadhaka up to this stage by gradual suspension of breath; mind then becomes un-mutative for a long time by just keeping Dhyana/attention on the incoming and outgoing breath. As Dhyana is continued, time comes when breath get suspended as the gap between incoming and outgoing breaths increases; Sadhaka is then with the spirit during this increased interval/gap; this finally leads to un-mutative stage of mind since mind gets its energy from breath only. This develops the mind and raises it to the unaware stage; thus silence and super conscious; intuition; the stateless state; just pour in gradually by Almighty's grace. This is the achievement by Sadhya Gayatri Sadhana similar to the other techniques. Furthermore, it can be said that by negation of mind, Buddhi (intellect), Chitta (conscious) and Ahankara/ego, one is near to soul. Added to this if consciousness is also diminished during meditation, there is ascend of soul to higher centers and its mergence occurs with the Supernal. This is the state of unison of microcosmic consciousness to the macrocosmic consciousness. Then there is no ego remains. Ego gets totally nullified and disappeared. In other words in this stage mind, consciousness and ego are in unison; the disappearance state. This is state beyond feeling and any action.

In this state breathe ceases to exist and suspended automatically. One can reach to this state with tranquil breath only. This is also achieved by Udana Prana technique. A man with haphazard and disturb breath cannot reach even the vicinity of the higher consciousness. There are more than 70 techniques to control the breath that can calm down mind, body and conscious to make a common human being a spiritual. The spirituality in a life of man is a purpose less purpose or in other world it is the highest purpose of life.

To make progress in the spirituality the basic requirement is the mental peace. For this spiritual aspirant must maintain the tranquil breath i.e. the breath must come and go from both the nostrils simultaneously. If this is maintained, one will feel relax and he will not be perturbed by fear and anxiety. Tranquil breath must be stable. It gives strength and increases Udana Prana in the human system that is the pre-requisite for the progress in spirituality. With tranquil breath Prana ascends through Brahmnadi very easily and with less effort. Most of the time for horizontal activity, breath transacts only through Inder Nadi. By Tranquil breath blissful stage comes naturally without efforts. This leads to generate 10 types of Nada in the system that makes the human body much healthier as compared to body that has disturbed and haphazard breath. Initially some efforts are needed to establish the tranquil breath but later on flow of tranquil breath becomes natural through the human system. Tranquil breath negates the divisible bio-lateral consciousness. It gives one pointed consciousness and concentration. Tranquil breath is a divine graceful breath. This gives silence to the mind and increase spiritual power, which is helpful in mergence with supernal. Furthermore, silence fulfills the system with harmony. This gives holy bath and removes heterogeneous polarity and helps to be one with the universe. Even in crisis, it gives peace and negates all selfish motives. It may give Sidhis to the Sadhaka and all selfish-motives in him cease to exist. No subjective attitude remains in a Sadhaka, he is always full of universal love and brotherhood. It finally leads to spiritual heights of skyness for mergence. One forgets that there is even cosmic consciousness and he becomes one with the cosmos. With higher spiritual conscious of Sadhaka, nothing can happen wrong with him on horizontal plane even if he loses awareness on the horizontal plane in the mundane activities.

In higher plane of super consciousness even if he gets momentary awareness of non-awareness, he becomes blissful with the grace of Almighty. Having forgotten awareness at the highest plane of super consciousness even for a few moments, he becomes SAKSHI CHAITNAYA from the state of Kutaksha Chaitanaya that leads him finally to Para Chaitanaya. He is then in absolute silence and the bliss he experiences in that stateless state is incomparable with any gain of the world. Similar experiences Sadhaka gains with the AUM technique.

So, in short any technique followed properly whether Udana Prana technique, AUM technique or Sandhya Gayatri technique, Sadhaka will ultimate experience the stateless state of incomparable bliss and his soul will merge in the Supernal and he will experience the state of absolute silence being in Savikalpa/ Nirvikalpa Samadhi.

Chapter 11

Types of Breaths, Tranquil Breath and their Importance

11.1 What are the different types of breaths and their effect on the human system?

Tranquil breath as has been explained in the earlier queries is the divine breath. Its appearance and disappearance depends on the divine power. It is not in the control of a human being. However, by modulation of physical health, and mental thinking and change in system vibrations, the tranquil breath can be established for a short duration. But, its longevity cannot be guaranteed.

Kula charkas, i.e. charkas below Manipura namely Muladhara and Swadhisthanam have gravitation pull and these chakras do not allow the upward journey of Udana Prana with Kundalini power and pull it back to the original mooring. But once the Manipura chakra is crossed then the effect of gravitational pull of Kula Chakras are seized to exist. In Kula chakra there is no awareness of Sakshi Chaitanya and Atam-sakshatkara/ God realization; it is not possible unless and until the transcendence of Kula chakra is achieved and life force reaches to Dhahara/Anahata chakra. Udana Prana is the life force at Muladhara, Swadhisthanam and Manipura chakras. At Dhahara/Anahata chakra there is a light of pure soul. This light of soul is self-abnegated at the Dhahara chakra. Jeeva coupled with soul/Atma is located at this chakra as Jeevatma. Kundalini is the sleeping force at the Kula chakra precisely at the Muladhara. Atman/soul light is the dormant; it is compiled with Jeeva at the Dharara chakra/ heart center. Jeeva/human being is conscious; it is in the manifested stage of awareness when Kundalini power and soul are in Samadhi/rest state at their respective locations/roots. Both soul and kundalini power remain in Samadhi/ sleeping state at their locations unless the Pranic forces do not awaken them. After the awakening of Kundalini power and ascent of soul to the higher centers, microcosm is merged with the macrocosm and super conscious state is achieved. When the kundalini power is awakened and soul ascends, the existing conscious/ aware state of the Sadhaka turns to unconscious/ unaware/mergence/Laya state and only then he enjoys the blessings of the Almighty.

The soul coupled/entangled with Jeeva termed as Jeevatma and it is the part of Shiva resting at the Dhahara/Anahata chakra. Kundalini being feminine power— Shakti rests at Muladhara chakra. They are merged in Maya and are in the gross aware state of complete rest under the influence of Maya. When the cause is created by the effect of Udana Prana, Shakti is awakened and merges with Shiva at the Dhahara chakra, and ascends to the Apex center. As they merge, both become unaware of the mergence, and decoupled from the effect of the Maya; they become the spirit power and the Sadhaka is blessed with the spiritual power. By the further ascendance of this Shiv-Shakti from Anahata Chakra to Visuddhi Chakra to Lambika Chakra onwards; they get purified and at the Ajna Chakra; Jeeva shades the effect of mind and gets united with the cause of creation; the Maya; after getting or as it get separated from the Jeevatma. Here at this location Jeeva and soul (Atman) are separated and are in face to face as soul/Atman and Jeeva. From this location onwards soul takes further journey to Unmani chakra in the Chida akasha after getting transformed into the divine light. The Pratyagatma, both soul and Jeeva i.e Jeevatma being always in face to face but in cohesion, split as Jeeva and Atman/ soul, is the first step of evolution of the spiritual aspirant to the spirituality at the Ajna chakra.

In a human system there are two basic Nadis connected with the two nostrils. Surya Nadi is connected with the right nostril and Chandra Nadi with the left nostril. Surya Nadi is atomic Nadi; it brings all divine qualities to the Sadhaka if it is opened; and one breathes freely through the right nostril. Moon Nadi is Jeeva Nadi; while freely breathing through this Nadi all sensory perceptions and emotional attitudes of the Sadhaka are strengthened. Thus, the left nostril breathing brings worldly perceptions and one is governed more by mind. But if both the nostrils are opened and one breathes in and breathes out through them, then Jeeva and Atma/soul of a person work with unison and homogeneity. All the good works are executed being in this state through such a person. Breathing in this pattern is a tranquil breathing. The tranquil breath is through the Brahma Nadi that is closely associated with both Surya Nadi and Moon Nadi, and is only possible by the wish of Almighty.

The activities of Jeeva are linked with emotions if they are governed by the Muladhara chakra; it is under the influence when only left nostril operates. Activities of Atman/soul are governed by Dhahara chakra when right nostril operates; then only the influence of soul/Atman is predominant on the Sadhaka. Dhahara chakra is the location of Jeevatma where it resides at peace. When left nostril operates, it shows that a person is in conscious state. He is in Maya in totality. On the contrary when right nostril operates, it indicates that a person is in Atmic/divine state and he is generally unconscious/unaware of the worldly mundane activities. Mind is mutative and thoughts of the mind go on changing with time depending on whether a person breathes from left nostril or right nostril. Some time he may behave like a saint and on another occasion his thoughts are governed by the animal instinct. If one is conscious of his mental state, he can modulate his thoughts by changing the breath pattern on altering the free flow of the air from one side of the nostril to the other side. Great Rishis/saints can change their breath pattern by their will. Such advanced Rishis/saints have symptoms of SAM YAMI LAKSHANA for controlling their thought pattern. This whole science is the science of tranquil breath. Tranquil breath is basically a variant constant and not the constant-constant. Disturbing thoughts can be controlled by changing the breath pattern by switching on left nostril breathing to the right nostril breathing. This is the yoga and this is called CHIT VRITI NRODHA that means one changes his emotional heart feeling and thought pattern as per his own will and requirement.

Dyana/meditation follows yoga. Nothing is better than Dyana in the system of yoga. One must meditate when breath is tranquil.

To make it tranquil one can open the close nostril by closing the open nostril and breath only through closed nostril forcefully. Doing this for one cycle or 9 times or two cycles of 9 times each, the closed nostril can be opened and one can establish the tranquil breath that is likely to make him peaceful in many respects. In this way tranquil breath is generated by itself; also, udana Prana helps the Sadhaka to be in meditation without much self-effort. After 5 cycles of horizontal breath, automatically 6th cycle will be of tranquil breath to calm down the human system. This changes the attitude of a person towards life and frequency of breath is reduced. This finally results in increasing the life span. Tranquil breath is bliss. It is also known as SAMYAMI SADHANA.

Tranquil breath gives light. Bhaj Govinda means to pray for light. Radha means continuation of emission of light. Light/Radha is always with Lord Krishna and this light/Radha rests at the Dhahara chakra/heart center as the Atman/soul that ascends to Ajna chakra and Chida akasha by yoga/meditation with the assistance of tranquil breath.

The above details give broadly different types of breaths and also the superiority of tranquil breath with the technique how to establish/re-establish it.

11.2 What are tranquil breath and how one gets and maintains it? What is the purpose and benefits of tranquil breath to a spiritual aspirant/Sadhaka?

Maya is a manifested form of God—the Almighty; the Brahma. Maya is called Brahma and Brahma in his manifested form is Maya. Human body/form is also Maya; the illusion. To take care of human body/form, continuously subtle energy is needed. This energy is drawn from the cosmos in the form of breath; one breathes about 10-15 times a minute (rate of breathing). Without this a Jeeva cannot survive even for a few moments. The breath supplies subtle energy to the physical body, which basically contains in subtle form fine elements i.e. earth (solid food), water, air, ether (Akasha-Pranic energy) and fire (heat energy) that regenerate the human system. Thus Brahma/Maya look after the human body through the subtle energy in the form of breath. Breath takes care of all the function of the body including physical, subtle and spiritual. Awareness of breath is a subtle spiritual technique that helps to ascend the Sadhaka's soul to the highest level to Supernal. This is nothing but the Sandhya Gayatri technique. This teaches a Sadhaka just to be with the breath and get dissolve into the breath and then breath ceases to exist and get suspended gradually; then one gets merge with the spirit; and a complete peaceful state ; a Silence State of God's realization is experienced.

The breath executes 99% functions of physical nature only. The breath can be basically divided into two broad categories firstly horizontal breath and secondly tranquil breath. Most of the times a human being takes horizontal breathe and does all worldly activities. Tranquil breath only helps him to do the transcendental activities – spiritual activities that create peace of mind. Horizontal breath nourishes senses; body; and accomplishes all earth born activities through the human form. On the contrary, tranquil breath helps mergence of soul with the Supernal. This breath tries to separate the consciousness gradually to help the soul for mergence with the Supernal. Tranquil breath enhances the spiritual functions but horizontal breath enhances mental functions, body functions, and all mundane worldly activities. Tranquil breath keeps a human being vigilant, alert and makes him Godly/Devik/Divine by intentions/nature. This magnetizes human cells with spiritual energy so as to facilitate the microcosm to merge with macrocosm.

Now, one understands clearly what is horizontal breath? And what is tranquil breath? Horizontal breath is that breath, which flows either through moon Nadi/left nostril or through sun Nadi/ right nostril. It goes on changing periodically and is attuned with the inner system of an individual. Tranquil breaths flow simultaneously without any resistance from both sun and moon Nadis i.e. left and right nostrils. Some times partly one nostril is working and sometimes both are partly opened. This is the state of partial tranquil breath but not the perfect tranquil breath.

In horizontal breath sometimes it is half of the earth element and rest half consists of other elements including water, fire, air and Akasha. Similarly if half is water constituent that rest are other elements put together. At time it is 50% Akasha elements and 50% all other elements consisting of earth, water, air and fire. But if there is perfect tranquil breath it consists of only Akasha elements and no other elements. Akasha element is generated directly from Udana Prana in the system, which ascends through spinal cord by Sushumna Nadi to the Kutakasha Chaitanya center to Sahasara and then to the Apex center. This creates spirituality in the human being and makes him divine personality. No other type of breath has this capacity to generate Udana Prana directly. Akasha element of breath and Udana Prana are easily converatable. Only Akasha element of breath can generate this and tranquil breath is full of Akasha element and nothing else. Tranquil breath is Shivasana breath. It is UTTAV MULAM and it is the only breath, which is AKASH MULAM and can go to Akasha. It is sky born breath. Where as horizontal breaths need to be compressed and strike in the Udana to generate Udana Prana. In tranquil breath, Akasha constituent is major so Udana Prana automatically appears in the system of the spiritual aspirant. Tranquil breath consisting of Akasha element is like engine and other elements of the breath are just boogies. They don't have capacity to drive where as tranquil breath with Akasha constituent is always in forefront to evolve the spiritual nature of the Sadhaka in an accelerated manner. It makes the Jeevatma a noble soul with time.

If the breath is not tranquil then residue is left in the nostrils. These residues are nothing but the earth/ Prithvi elements/Tattva. Running nose of a person indicates that he has more of water Tattva/ element. Blood coming from nostril indicates Agni Tattva that shows excessive of heat in the body. If the breath is tranquil, it prepares the body in a natural way for higher journey. Mind, intellect, consciousness get prepare due to tranquility of the system to take up higher journey and become spiritual gradually in course of time if breath is tranquil most of time. Tranquil breath is yoga Kriya. Every 6th breath cycle after 5 horizontal breath cycles is partially tranquil and gives the divine effect to the human system and keeps his mind generally under peace. Sometimes after 9 horizontal breath cycles, one tranquil breath cycle appears. If one spends more time in AUM japa or other spiritual practices, the frequency of the appearance of earth/horizontal breaths are minimized and frequency of tranquil breaths are increased. If one sleeps with the tranquil breath i.e. with more Akasha elements then most likely when he gets up he will be having the similar tranquil breath. Tranquil breath is the precursor for evolution and to make progress in meditation. Tranquil breath acts as a fuel for Udana Prana and helps Udana Prana to ascend from Kula chakra. After ascending the life force/Udana Prana unto Kutakasha Chaitanaya, the role of breath is diminished. At this Triveni junction, inner soul takes over and performs onward ascends to Apex center. At Turiya State and Super Turiya state/ super conscious state, there is no role of tranquil breath. The out come of tranquil breath is to give mental peace; it gives transcendence that pays dividend at this stage apart from the generation of Udana Prana.

Tranquil breath gives Sat Agni to the Sadhaka. It gives Prana Shakti and Chida Agni to the Sadhaka to ascend up to Triveni junction within no time with Sahaj Bhava without any struggle and less efforts on the horizontal plane. The above explains the origin, purpose and benefit of tranquil breath to a human being and particularly to spiritual aspirant for ascending of Prana and mergence of soul with Supernal.

11.3 How to generate tranquil breathe in the system for the spiritual evolution?

Tranquil breath is a God gifted breath. Only this type of breath can take a spiritual aspirant for vertical journey; a sky ward journey; for mergence of soul with the Supernal. After 5 cycles of horizontal breath, there are chances for the 6th cycle to be vertical breath i.e. tranquil breath so that the agitated mind can have some peace to deal with the worldly activities; otherwise life of a common man can become full of misery in all respects. So God by its own natural way helps to maintain the minimum level of peace and harmony in human life so that peace prevails even in Tamasik and Rajasik activities performed by him.

If the elemental/horizontal breath gets irritated due to unpalatable physical or mental activity on horizontal or subtle plane then there will not be tranquil breath even after five cycles of elemental breaths. And some times when there is tranquil breathe and if suddenly mind gets irritated and gets pre-occupied with horizontal thoughts then it is automatically crashed and elemental breath takes over. Basically tranquil breath is naturally unnatural or unnaturally natural breath. If the mind is peaceful by Dhyana and yoga practices, then the breath will be tranquil; or in other words tranquil breath brings easily the Dhyana state of mind; otherwise one has to struggle; and this state may not come easily. When there is no tranquil breath, there are chances of frustration in mind and occurrences of different types of subjective mental problems. It is restless state and even suicidal tendency can come if the cycle of tranquil breath is not repeated automatically after 6 or 12 cycles of horizontal or elemental breathes. Blood pressure of a person is under control by the tranquil breath. If the automatic cycle of tranquil breath is normal, the problem of high B. P. or low B. P. generally do not exist, which are related to mental stress. Heart lungs function properly if the sequence of tranquil breath is automatically maintained by nature. Emotions and undue thoughts do not disturb and a person generally feels healthy by his own. But on the contrary if horizontal cycles of the breaths are in excess then consciousness is not properly maintained. Also, blood is not purified due to blood pressure problems; and cholesterol in the blood increases since the unpurified blood circulates in the system. Generally, cholesterol problem is closely linked with the residual of unpurified blood, which impure blood leaves on the walls of the artilleries due to its circulation; this is not properly purified in lungs by blood pressure issues, which are directly linked with the absence of tranquil breath cycles of the breathing system.

Even by Mantra recitation tranquil breath cycle can be maintained. This cleans the system and allows proper rest period to heart without getting them worn out fast; and adequate absorption of oxygen by lungs is maintained. In short, tranquil breath has the mysterious effect on the major human systems and their longevity with out any problems.

Now the question arises, if the tranquil breath cycle is not normal, what to do and how one can increase number of tranquil breathe cycles to be in peace and stress free for most of time. This can be done by the forceful means if the breath does not flow from both the nostrils equally. The side, which is blocked, one must allow to pass air through that by closing the other nostril. Thus by 9 times or 18 times taking the breath from the blocked nostril, this may open it partially and breath may flow from both the nostrils simultaneously and equally. Thus tranquil breath can be established and the cycles of horizontal breaths can be broken. One must become the master of breath; must be conscious to be mentally and physically healthy for living in the horizontal plane; so that one can make the vertical sky ward journey to probe the unknown. It is the basic duty of a human being to be with the un-known; to be with the un-manifested world as with the known – manifested world. Both are the two shores of the same Almighty. Manifested matter cannot exist without the un-manifested part/space in it. The Maya being manifested and God and divine being are un-manifested; and both co-exist together. We must bow to both of them for our travel and success in this world.

Mantra vibration by its recitation is the precursor of the tranquil breath and the seed of the tranquil breath. One can get into tranquil breath by Mantra recitation; and can easily become part of this elemental breath, which is ground-ward and earth-born breath. By the force of Mantra, the linkage of horizontal breaths can be broken to get the tranquil breath. Even if one fails number of time to establish the tranquil breathe, but finally he is likely to succeed to establish tranquil breath. Even then one can turn back to the elemental breath cycles and have same animal tendency; emotional disturbances; and again he may act as per disturbed feeling of mind and intellect. This is the Maya/illusion and it is all-powerful. One must admit and bow the Maya and take his blessings to be peaceful; he must try again to establish tranquil breath to succeed. Tranquil breath can be disturbed within no time/ instantaneously; but horizontal breath is very powerful and cannot be defeated early and easily.

Practically, for a yogi, who lives in the mundane world and practice spirituality for higher awareness, both tranquil breath and elemental breath exist together most of the time; he tries to be conscious for horizontal activities and direct his energies for vertical travel simultaneously; he tries to maintain balance between horizontal and vertical breaths. If both tranquil and element breath co-exist then the Sadhaka's understanding is beyond understanding. His mind is conscious with I ness; it ness; and my ness; and at the same time he can direct his energies for divinity. He is in psycho-spiritual state; and most of the time he is conscious even in dreams. Only by the grace of Almighty and His blessings, his breath remains tranquil and he maintains peace within him. But, at time, one has to pray for peace and tranquil breath. Man is totally helpless to achieve any success of any kind in his life without tranquil breath. Only by divine grace, he is gifted with higher perceptions. With his higher perceptions, having tranquil breath, his soul is detached from Jeeva for higher journey. However, when breath is elemental, Jeeva is coupled with the soul. The soul is librated only when the basic requisite of tranquil breath is attained besides other advanced means and faculties. Without the grace of Guru, Almighty and blessing of the Cosmic Mother, nothing can be achieved. All techniques and exercises are just futile without any purposeful gain. Any time one can be thrown in Maya, just being unaware of. Moreover, when he gets awareness he is surprised why he did all that way. Intellect/Buddhi become just full of mist and he is caught unaware of by Maya by elemental breaths. When he responds, he is failed to understand that Maya was so powerful that he was caught unaware and acted as per the command of Maya. There is nothing certain in this world. Anything can happen any time. There is no guarantee for any mode of behavior. God catches us unaware with mystery for good or bad to be in His panorama, in His grace as play. Being, even at the threshold of the unknown, everything can be spoiled without His ray of grace and blessings. Tranquil breath is just the pretext but there is no surety of any kind. Any time one can fall. X-factor – the Maya is so powerful that at times one's divine experience will be futile. And nothing could be done. No theories could be made and no procedure could be laid. Every thing is by the grace of Maya and we must propitiate Maya to succeed on any path. Maya is Brahma and Brahma is Maya. Without his blessings and grace, the path will be full of mist although prayers, Mantra recitation, yoga and tranquil breath are the means to succeed. However, every means is powerless without His desires and wishes.

In conclusions, it can only be said that the tranquil breath is divinity and it comes with divine grace only. The techniques and means to get tranquil breath are just the exercises but the driving force to bless the tranquil breath or to withdraw it is all by the mercy of the Almighty. His grace and mercy are the only stairs to climb and other are just the means.

Chapter 12

Lord Sri Medha Dakshina Murthi and his Tatva

12.1 What are the backgrounds; religious importance and significance of multi dimensional worship able Lord Om Sri Medha Dakshina Murthy? What is "Dakshina Murthy Tatva"?

Shri Medha Dakshina Murthy is well known particularly in southern part of India. In northern India Ishwara is considered the supreme, omnipresent, omniscient and Kaltita/beyond time. Shri Medha Dakshina Murthy and Ishwara are the synonyms of the same omnipresent force of the universe and cosmos. Nothing and nobody is above them. All known cosmic forces and worshiper deities of the universe worship Ishwara or Om Meda Dakshina Murthy. If a Sadhaka/spiritual aspirant during his spiritual practices gets the glimpses/feels of "silence" in his own Chida akasha, he is considered to be the beloved and blessed devotee of Medha Dakshina Murthy and Ishwara. They are the real pillars of "silence" and without their blessings to achieve or even to step in the mental "silence" are much far away from the contemplation. From silence all the power is emancipated. To be in "silence" is the art and being "silent" is like; as if in unison with Medha Dakshina Murtthy; the lord—the Ishwara. It is the highest achievement that a Sadhaka can dream and imagine.

Dakshina is a direction of Yama -- an end; an end is "silence"; and being silent is like, being in omnipresent. So even to follow the direction towards a silence zone makes a Sadhaka powerful and to be in that, makes him as the image of Ishwara; and he is adored accordingly.

Furthermore DA (Dhakshina Amurthy) means that which is "KSHI" — the creator and giver of light. This means that the world has Aadi (beginning); Madhya (middle); and Antah (end); and Dakishna Murthy is beyond Aadi, Madhya and Antah.In other words world is mutative and goes on changing with time and finally gets collapsed. Dakshina Murthy is the cause of creation; it is also the cause of its dissolution. The word Murthy symbolized as "Murth", the face that can be interpreted as direction. And Murthy means, which can be recognized. Through Maya recognition is easier. Where as Amurthy gives direction to be followed for spiritual evolution that will finally leads to "Yama" as an end, which means towards silence zone. Dhakshina Murthy is ego-less and beyond many-ness, so Dhakshina Murthy is full of humility. Dhakshina Murthy symbolizes to give a direction for spiritual up-liftment to spiritual aspirant that takes him at the end to the silence zone before mergence in to the Sahasrara. Hence it is Dakshina Murthy before Sahasrara, and beyond Sahasrara it is Dhakshina Amruthy. This, if achieved, is the highest achievement of Sadhaka's life i.e. to get mergence in Supernal; and later then emergence from Supernal; and be with the Ishwara as the Jeewan Mukta. In addition, Dakshina Murthy is a source of ultimate and it is the source light. . There is no comparison of such a highest meaning with any existing word in any language as that of Dakshina Murthy— the Ishwara.

After going through ancient literature in more details, it has been established that there are five Brahmas. Sada Shiva is the first Brahma. In Sada Shiva all directions of five faces of Brahma is contained. Three faces are of Brahma, Vishnu and Maheshwara of the Sada Shiva that have specific roles in the cosmos i.e. creation, maintenance or sustenance and dissolution. The fourth face of Sada Shiva — Dakshina Murthy comes in the end since he has no function to perform and express; Dakshina Murthy is always silent. His function continues in time memorials i.e. in timelessness or for several crores/millions of years. The dissolution/ withdrawal of entire creation are by Dakshina Murthy; and this creation is entirely a play of Dakshina Murthy. He knows it is His play. Brahma and

Vishnu are creator and sustainer by him. Dakshina Murthy Swarupa i.e. Rudra and Maheshwara are Mouni/silent. They exist mostly in silence, meditative mood and communicate in silence. In addition, Dattatreya is symbol of union of Brahma, Vishnu and Mahesh and the fourth Brahma united with these three is Dakshina Murthy.

Dakshina as illustrated above is the end, means void. This illustrates that nothing is there. Nothing in void can be seen by the physical eyes or by imagination. In other words Dakshina means beyond and beyond i.e. void and silence.

If one turns towards east, his right hand goes to south and left hand goes to north. It is very vivid form here that when one pays his complete attention towards the Almighty, his actions must be pure, right and radiant. Only this will lead to Dakshina; the south; and the abode of silence. And from silence spiritual aspirant can draw positive divine energy for right actions in all the multi dimensional planes and even on the horizontal plane. Thus, he becomes pure in thoughts, words and deeds that can lead him to get mergence in the silence; and finally in the abode of Supernal. On the contrary, the deeds on the horizontal plane take him to left direction away from silence and there will not be any end to all this. All Rajasik activities of the horizontal plane will be in progress but with various ups and downs.In the end, doer will find himself in misery and move away and away from silence i.e. from the path of Dakshina Murthy.

When there is desire of Kameswara; then there is a presence of Shiva – Shakti. Above Shiva and Shakti there is an arena of Dakshina Murthy — a complete union — the abode of absolute silence. There is no impression left to Sada Shiva by the mergence of Shiva – Shakti. This mergence is Dakshina Murthy i.e. the silence, which is the end/ultimate and this is called Ishwara. Ishwara means Panch Brahma Swarupini i.e. Sada Shiva, Dakshina Murthy, Brahma, Vishnu and Maheswara. That is Lalita beyond Vak and impression. That is abode of absolute silence. Therefore Dakshina Amruthy is equal to Lalita. Furthermore, it can be illustrated that when one is aware of Srishti Karma, one is united in Medha, which is the light. That light is completely aware of; and it is Sampoorna; and it is silent as Dakshina Murthy. This Guyana — the knowledge, is beyond all the existing knowledge i.e. Guyana/knowledge, Agyana/ignorance and Pragnayana. All these are by the blessings of Lord Dakshina Murthy. It is source of all happiness. Vignayana is the secular knowledge that can be proved on the material plane by horizontal means. This is only integral knowledge, which is based on the series of knowledge. But Medha is combined and above such kind of knowledge's. Medha is pure and is on the intuitive plane. There is no logic for this pure light intuitive knowledge. This is the knowledge that one gets in silence only. This knowledge is by Medha Dakshina Murthy.

Medha Dakshina Murthy is always young 16 years old. This knowledge is always alive, and it is above all and cannot become redundant with time as being an integral knowledge. This knowledge is Shodasi i.e. of sixteen Bijas i.e. of 16 Kalas. It symbolizes Laya—the Savikalpa Samadhi — the mergence of soul with the Supernal. It is super conscious/Turiya state. It is said for Megha Dakshina Murthy being always as 16 years old that "Vrudhaha Sishya Yuva Guruhu" i.e. young guru and old disciple. All Braham Rishis including Trimurthy i.e. Brahma, Vishnu and Rudra and rest of them in the cosmos beg for the blessings of Medha Dakshina Murthy in the form of Maha Chaitanya i.e. super consciousness, which gets transformed as Para Chaitanya -- the divine light— as it ascends in Chida akasha. Only by the blessings of this divine light, Yama state (the end state) i.e. abode of silence can be stepped in and that makes the spiritual aspirant "silent" for years together. This silent state is beyond awareness. It is Medha state. Medha is not being awareness as present or absent. It is beyond time i.e. the timeless state – a void – complete silence and state within the super Self. On this supreme level one is in Srushti karna Pragnyana i.e. Samhara Karma i.e. in state of complete knowledge and happiness. It is Medha i.e. it is light that knows everything. Only He can, if likes to continue the survival of living being or can withdraw i.e. can initiate Pralaya: So Medha contains both "life" and "no life". He is called Medha Dakshina Murthy when He continues 'life" in this universe; as well as Dakshina Amurthy when it withdraws "life'. If this is allowed to happen, it is called the state beyond mergence i.e. Amurthy. Medha is also

Lalita i.e. "Sarwatita iti Lalita" ; under this state Medha is female. Medha along with Pragnyana is male as Brahma or creator. Both of them have no Karya, no Karma so they are beyond action and are in the abode of silence. Thus that which is beyond cause and effect of expression is Medha. He has no source. All the Brahmas prostrate to him. So it may be said that Dakshina Murthy is "Pum Rupa" of Sri Lalita. It is that source light, which is sitting to create as cause and effect; and thus the continuation of Jeeva's manifestation and multiplication goes on; and also Medha has a capacity of withdrawal and the dissolution; and then under this state Pralaya comes.

Furthermore, the Vata Vruksha is a creation i.e. by Vata / Pranic energy every jeeva is created and takes the form of body. So body of each jeeva is treated as Vata Vruksha. Mula is the cause of creation. Also, Karmic desire is the cause; this subjugates the compiling of male and female for reproduction. Similarly Srushti Mula indicates Vignayana and Pragnayana, which is Medha – the silence; it is the basis of all knowledge; including integral, spiritual and cosmic.

Sada Shiva is Karna Brahma of five stages of creation including Brahma, Vishnu, Mahesh and Dakshina Murthy from the Self i.e. Sada Shiva. The Sada Shiva is the basic infinite cause of cosmos i.e. its creation and withdrawal in totality.

MANTRA

Om Sri Namo Vata Moola Vasine Namo

Bhagawate Dakshina Murtaye Mahyam

Medham pragnyanam prayaccha swaha

Prakata Gayatri is Sandhya Devi. A Prakata Gayatri is Medha Dakshina Murthy.

It is Raja Aushada. It helps to get into Mouna – silence. After that there is no need. It can make one sit in any nest one belongs to. It eliminates disturbing factors, conscious or unconscious. To make sure one gets early into his nest.

Vata is Asmadha, Urdhva is Moolam or the mother root of all creation. His place is at the Brahma Randhra.

"I am doing this to give you the boon to know you more, you to have more knowledge. Make you Pragnayanam to be given you again, and not to be misused by you", This is purpose of the Mantra.

Chapter 13

Self, Soul/Atma, Kundalini Power, Udana Prana, Jeevatma and their Role in Spiritual Evolution

13.1 What is Self? What is soul/Atman and Jeevatma? What is the basic difference among Self, Soul and Jeevatma? Why there is lot of ambiguity in the literature on the use of these terms?

Self is a force, which carries out every function in a human life. Self is one's own egoism. Without self nothing can be done. Self seems to be uplifted when individual gains. Self is only hurt under miserable conditions. Self drives us. Self is present in all individuals. Without self no activity can be carried out. One praises self and one blames self under different conditions. The Self is omnipotent force. Self is God within us. Then why a human being does wrong and shameful act? When self is God within us; and it is assumed and perceived that the God; the same Self; exists in each one of us. If a good thing is done, one appreciates that the Almighty has done; and also if one does wrong act still the Almighty; the Self; is blamed.

How the Self, the part and parcel of the omnipresent, omnipotent force does a wrong act? He cares for all the living being then why the Self, the God, within us is to be blamed? There is some dilemma in this complex understanding. And, this needs to be deeply understood and appreciated. For example, as petrol/gasoline is the same to drive each automobile irrespective of its make, shape and size, similarly each human being is governed and managed by the same Self irrespective of his name and form. As without gasoline, no vehicle can run so no human being can survive without self. If gasoline/petrol makes a vehicle to run and meets with the accident, shall the gas/petrol to be blamed or the vehicle is to be blamed? No body blames either petrol and nor the vehicle. Only the driver is blamed in all these happenings/conditions. Similarly the self does every activity, like gas/petrol in the vehicles to drive; to act; but still like petrol – the Self is not responsible. By our wrong perception, our ignorance makes the Self-responsible; for all our good and bad acts particularly the bad/wrong acts.

We say/admit the Self does every activity and without self, nothing can be done. Because He; the Self; is the part/replica of God in us; and He is the driving force behind every activity. It is true that He/Self does every thing but still dilemma is that He/Self does nothing. He; the Self; is just the blind and powerful force of Almighty in us. Without Him nothing is undoubtedly possible but for every act of ours; He; the Self/ Almighty is not responsible. What a strange paradox! He/Self does every activity but does not take the responsibility of any of His act. It means there is some other linkage through whom the Self and human egoism works. That linkage needs to be perceived and purified to perform the best acts by the Self since self as a free will; it can adopt any path right or wrong. There is some other force that guides its or the work of self. As petrol drives the vehicle, but does not show the direction. So, it is just the doer; but a force that does all the activities of the human being is guided by another mysterious force.

Jeevatma in the human being drives the Self. It is the human's pure and mixed soul so all the right and wrong activities are carried out by the direction and instructions of Jeev- atman but by the force of self, which's the part /replica of the Almighty. Subtly it is rather very complex and difficult to conceive. To have a very clear picture is beyond discussions, logics and apprehension at times.

Psychologically human senses, i.e. eyes, nose, tongue, skin, ear are closely interrelated with the mind and intellect. And they all influence the jeeva/living-being or in other words Jeevatma/soul of the living-being; and all the horizontal and vertical activities are carried out as if Atman; the soul; as the Self, which is the image/ part of Almighty in us, is executing because that is the only executive force in us similar to gas or petrol in the automobiles. This is perceived since after death all the senses are in tact and which leaves body/human form is Self or Atman/soul. Although, the pure self is not the doer/executor; but it is considered to be the basically doer/executor of all the activities.

In general, senses influence the mind. Based on the whim and fancy of the powerful mind; jeevatma; and the mixed Self (with pure and impure virtues); positioned at Dhahara chakra located at the heart center; acts. However, intellect being more subtle and nearer to mind can control/govern the mind to some extent. Atman/ soul; the pure Self; a pure divine light; is not able to effect and convince the mutative mind, which is always under the strong influence of powerful Maya-illusion. So, basically human life under the influence of strong mutative mind revolves around senses in the horizontal plane and human egoism is developed to such a high order that a human considers that Self (mixed Self) is his egoistic power; and through this egoism, his activities are governed till the time his egoism is hurt by the impact of egoism of others. This leads to fight, quarrels, and execution of wrong deeds without any basis of understanding; and finally the Self is blamed as if Self; the Almighty; is responsible for all such sub-standard and inhuman activities under the influence of greediness, desires, anger, sex and so on. It looks Maya; the most powerful force is getting done all such acts by the Self, through the Self. It is all Maya since Maya is considered as Brahma. As if Self; the God is responsible for all this. Basically Jeevatma under the influence of Maya is the doer and responsible for all executions.

Now the bottom line is that the senses must be controlled by the mind. Mind must be made strong, greater and finally the greatest to control the senses. Preaching's/instructions of Lord Krishna are to be followed as per the third chapter of Geeta. Desires must be sublimated; since man minus desire is God. By overcoming the desires; by control of senses; by the self- restrains and by practice of yoga; and by the grace of Guru and Mahaavatar Babaji, the Vasanas are purified; thus the mind is controlled. Intellect becomes sharp and thus with all this Jeeva/living being is uplifted by its purity. By ascend of life force through heart center, the Atman; the soul; and the Jeevatma reaches the Ajna chakra. Here the Jeeva gets separated from Jeevatma. The pure Atman/soul stays at the Ajna chakra. The pure Atman is Self without egoism, desires, Vasanas and inclination of the senses. This/ pure soul transform into the divine light by years of spiritual practice and mind gets dissolved into the soul; the Self; that ascends up to Apex center and merges with Supernal. The soul, pure Atman i.e. the Self at the Ajna chakra under the influence of pure mind and intellect does only good activities. Such activities done by human being are divine and are without the tint of selfishness. At Ajna chakra soul is a pure Self. At Dhahara, soul/Atman is Jeevatma. Activities carried out by jeevatma being at Dhahara chakra are not the pure activities done by the Self. Jeevatma in its pure state becomes Self only at Ajna chakra and not at the lower charkas. Jeevatma is wrongly termed as self and considered like an Almighty; carrying out right and wrong activities. These are basically done by jeevatma under the influence of distorted impure mind and senses and not by the Self. Self is God; pure soul; it cannot be directed by impure mind since when it becomes pure then only soul ascends to Ajna to Sahasara by getting transformed into divine light and not before that by any other means. So Self; the pure soul; the part/image of Almighty is to be worshipped. The mis-interpretation of self in the literature has caused different confusions and discussions on this subject. Basically it is Jeevatma that is responsible for all mixed activities and not the Self, which is a part of Almighty.

13.2 What is the role of Kundalini power, Udana Prana, Jeevatama and Atman/soul in the spiritual evolution of a spiritual aspirant/Sadhaka?

There are five types of elemental Prana in a human body. As the air/ Pawan by the process of breathing goes through the nostrils inside the human system, it gets converted into Shavas/breath at the Visuddhi chakra. This breath after taking the energy from the soul at the Dhahara chakra is converted into Prana. However, only a part of the breath is transformed into Prana. This Prana is further transformed to Samana, Vayana, Apana and Udana Pranas. By the close interaction and impact of various Pranas, Udana Prana is formed. It has maximum of sky content and only this Prana can ascend. It is transformed into the divine light after perfect/partial purification in the different chakras of the human system before it reaches at the Ajna chakra. Udana Prana is Brahman. Other Pranas are manifestation of Maya for the Jeevatma. They contain more percentage of earth, water, fire and air. Only Udana Prana is full of ether and can take sky ness path for mergence with Supernal after transformations on the ascending path through various chakras.

Basically by the yoga practices Udana Prana is generated in the human system. By Puraka, Rechaka and Kumbhaka practices of yoga, transformation of Udana Prana takes place from the existing Pranas. Two Pranas namely Prana and Vayana like Pandvas are on side; above the navel in the human system, where as Samana and Apana like Kauravas on the lower side; below the navel center. The close interaction and impact of these Pranas like the Kurkshetra war leads to generate the light out of this mutual rubbing. This light is named as Udana Prana. As Kauravas and Pandvas are born by the supreme will of Lord Krishna so these four Prana are born by the soul light existing at the Dhahara/Anahata chakra. Udana Prana/light is the outcome/effect of interaction of these Pranas. However, the basic cause of appearance of Udana Prana is the soul (force/part of Almighty) residing in the human system. The close interaction of these Pranas separates Udana Prana automatically. This function is independent by itself as the out come of the action less action of the different Pranas.

This Udana Prana immediately after formation interacts with Swadhisthanam chakra, being nearest to navel center. Here by the warmth/ fire/Agni effect of Manipura; Udana Prana is purified and absorbed by the awareness of fire/Agni. Thus, the flame of fire, containing Udana Prana spreads all around and interacts with Muladhara chakra being closest to Manipura and Swadhisthanam. The Kundalini power lying as three and half inch coiled in Muladhara, in a Samadhi state, is awakened by the heat and light of Udana Prana. The Kundalini power lies in transcended and dormant state under the effect of Maya until and unless it is pushed by the force of the Udana Prana. As it is pushed; it rises like a snake, which was resting in 3 ½, inches turns coils at Muladhara, and then goes to Manipura charka through the Swadhisthanam along with the light/energy of Udana Prana. In this chakra under the effect of water effect of Swadhisthanam, Kundalini power tends to become Sattvik; it gets purified like Mani and cools down. Further, kundalini power along with Udana Prana that has converted partially into the divine light ascends to Dhahara chakra. The interaction of ascending energy at the Dhahara and Manipura chakras continue gradually; and finally the divine light of Udana Prana and Kundalini is absorbed by the soul residing at Dhahara. As a pure soul light from Dhahara chakra, this energy ascends to Visuddhi and Lambika chakras. Residual Prana remaining with this energy loses its Pranic function at Visuddhi chakra. Other ingredient of light i.e. yellow, blue, red etc., are filtered in the Lambika chakra, and purest of the pure divine light ascends at the Ajna chakra. Here there is no Udana Prana, no Kundalini and no other gradients remain; and all are merged in oneness in the pure divine light of the soul.

If soul has carried along with it Jeeva, then there are chances of vision and memories at the Ajna chakra due to the presence of Jeeva and not only the exclusive light of the Atman/soul. It means Jeevatma has ascended to this location along with the pure soul/ Atman from the Dhahara chakra. If there is pure soul then the Atman Sakshatkara i.e. Self-realization is possible at this location since it is the stage of the opening of third eye. However, Self-realization gradually starts manifesting/ reflecting in the Sadhaka's awareness with time if this practice is continued for years under the blessings of Sat Guru.

From the Ajna chakra, light spreads in the Chida akasha/Gagana and Sadhaka experiences awakening/dream/deep slumbering/ Sushupati/ and then Turiya/transcendence Sandhya states. In presence of the Jeeva, there prevails superfine awareness but if Jeeva is separated and only soul/Atman ascends then there does not remain any awareness and it is called the Turiya state/ transcendental state.

Turiya is the blissful state. However, Illusion of bliss is different than that of the blissful state. In this blissful state there is no ego, no kundalini, no Prana, no Jeeva and only there is the presence of pure soul that gives the divine light. So, blissful state is a state of mergence in pure light with supernal. Only at this stage soul is liberated. No function is required to be performed in the stage. It is state of Turiya Tita, which is beyond Turiya. No one can describe this state. If one can describe and say, it means he was in Maya - illusion and not in mergence; Turiya Tita/ and blissful state.

The above clarifies the role of Pranas, Kundalini, Jeevatma, Jeeva and soul in subtle manner in the spiritual evolution of a Sadhaka/spiritual aspirant.

13.3 Why there are number of pit falls in yoga Sadhana/ spiritual practices for the beginners particularly when the life force/Udana Prana tries to ascend from the lower charkas namely Muladhara and Swadhisthanam?

Before a Sadhaka takes up the practices of yoga, all the Chakras in his system are closed/sealed. Every Chakra has its original characteristics. When the chakras are blossom by the passage of Kundalini power/Udana Prana, specific dormant tendencies of a Sadhaka awake in the process. For the beginners, as the Udana Prana is generated in the navel region, it goes to the Manipur Chakra that has its seat in the navel center in the spinal cord. It is the fire/ Agni region. Udana Prana under the influence of fire of the Manupura Chakra and under the effect of Swadhisthanam Chakra gets vaporized and its vapors spread all around and pierce through Muladhara Chakra and its surrounding regions. The Kundalini power in the subtle stage of Samadhi resting in the coccyx at Muladhara region as the three and half-inch coil awakens by the immense pressure of Udana Prana and its heat energy. It then tries to pierce through Muladhara Chakra and gradually ascends through Swadhisthana Chakra. The entire earth bound concealed tendencies become active in the mind of a beginner Sadhaka. Earth bound tendencies like sex/procreation, attraction for varieties of tasty food, greed, anger, pride and attachments etc., manifest to the highest level depending on the potentiality of the tendencies. Some times Sadhaka is not able to control the manifested urge that forces him to indulge in these activities through the lowest possible extent/ level. He becomes Deha abhimani/proud of physical body and profoundly gets attached with instinctual desires to fulfill them. But, gradually, if he continues his Sadhana/spiritual practices, these tendencies die down and get nullified as the Udana Prana gets purified under the fire of Manipura and Swadhisthana chakras, and on passing through these chakras. But this stage of initial evolution is very dangerous and one can become prey of negative tendencies for a long time till their effect is subsided with time.

As the time passes and if the Sadhaka continues his Sadhana with sincerity he may become the master of eight Sidhis of yoga that make him Mahatma, the great soul with time for the external world. Inside his Jeevatma gets purified and he passes comfortably from the four stages of evolution i.e. he may transcend easily Wakeful stage, Dream, Sushupati and Turiya/transcendental State and finally he may step into Savikalpa to Nirvikapa Samadhi. He becomes one with the divine light in the Turiya state before mergence with the Supernal. In the process of evolution he becomes Sthiita Pragnya. He gets involved more in divine activities that projects his inherent talents but his talents don't show his egoism of any kind.

On the contrary, in the initial stages of evolution when energies are mostly concentrated in Muladhara and Swadhisthanam; he has mixed instinct and free nature; his consciousness is also mixed. Depending on the mental tendency and mixed consciousness, the decisions he takes of life, may prove to be self contradictory with time. He is more under the effect of Maya, the illusion; his nature will be very transient. It may be Tamasic, Rajasik or Sattvik; every thing is unpredictable for him in the initial stages. His actions may not show consistency since all his actions are governed by the invoked tendencies in the lower charkas. He may himself be surprised for his own behavior sometimes being Sattvik and sometimes highly Tamasik. This is because of the transient stage of evolution. Sometimes such a beginner aspirant talks of himself and may talk futile. His actions cannot be predicated unless his Udana Prana stabilizes in the Manipura and Dhahara chakras. In the beginning he is SKAMA SADHAKA and follows subtle ego path; he can curse to the fellow beings with prejudices and Raga to fulfill his own wordly desires. But, gradually as he ascends in the path of spirituality, he becomes desire less. He becomes NISHKAMA SADHAKA. He enjoys to be with himself and to be near to his soul as much as possible. Then his destination is neither cause and nor effect. He gets fused in himself as if milk is mixed with milk, which then cannot be separated. Thus he supersedes his bad desires and even he does not show/project any caliber, which he posses.

As he climbs up in the path of vertical journey, he needs to control his mind by Dhayana. He is neither to negate his own mind and nor to provoke it. By this his mind becomes strong. He needs to train his mind with positive thoughts and philosophy of the art of correct living and dealings. He must train his mind to explain: why desires of any kind; death waits at the doorstep that gives him perfect peace; awareness to detachment; contemplate on the satisfaction what Almighty has granted/ given. That way, if mind is trained, it becomes one pointed and this is all needed for prelude to Dhyana for the forward vertical journey so that ego, subconscious, and desires do not become obstacles in the path of spiritual evolution. Thus, a Sadhaka in the path of evolution at the Swadhisthana and Muladhara can train his mind initially so that ego gets dissolved and attitudes towards desires become nullified and their futility is understood. So that onward journey becomes natural throughout till the mergence takes place.

In short, miseries during initial evolution are natural under the effect of Maya and latent tendencies. Gyana/knowledge is required to develop the conscious attitude so that the problems are tolerated as the natural phenomenon. Grace of Almighty does help to the real Sadhakas in this path. Prayers are the divine boon to the Sadhakas to come out from such obstacles, which is the best possible way to take up this onward journey for mergence with the Supernal.

Chapter 14

Pranas, Their Role and Vertical Travel of Prana for Self Realization

14.1 What are the various types of Pranas and their role in Self-realization? At the time of death, which is the locations, Prana can leave the physical body? And on what conditions these locations depend?

There are total ten types of Pranas in the human body. Out of which five are very significant. They have very specific role to make the human body/form healthy and at the same time help the Sadhaka for mergence with the Supernal. The importance Pranas are: Prana, Vyana, Samana, Udana Prana, Apana, Naga, Karma, Kurkara, Devdata and Dhanjaya.

Prana is the part of breath. The air, a human being breath contains Prana Shakti along with oxygen and other constituents. How this Pranic power exists in the atmosphere? arounds us; is a spiritual, scientific and a mysterious mystery. There is no valid explanation to explain this mystery. It is a divine miracle. One can live without food and drink for quite some time, but not without the breath and the Pranic energy. Human being is declared dead when he cannot breath. The breath is the only communication with the cosmos i.e. with the external world. It is the only practical linkage between inner and outer surroundings. Inner system is badly affected if the outer surroundings are not healthier. After the breath is taken inside through nostrils, it becomes Shavasa; Prana is separated at the Visuddhi chakra at throat region from the Shavasa. This Prana is further transformed in Vayana Prana at the heart region at Dhahara chakra. From here it gets distributed in the human system and keeps the system and vital organs working by the Pranic energy.

The same Pranic energy of the breath is transformed into Samana Prana at the Manipura and Swadhisthanam region. The Vyana Prana distributes the Pranic energy carried by the Samana Prana. Depending on the needs of the organs, Samana Prana is distributed. After this Apana Prana is generated in the lower organs from the vital Prana. Apana Prana helps for secretion and the functioning of the excrete system. The force of Apana Prana removes excreta of body. These Pranas are self generated in the system by the Pranic energy of the breath and is automatically distributed in the system by the auto system.

Apart from the above four types of Pranas, as discussed, Udana Prana is required to be generated in the system by the close interaction/impact of Vyana Prana, vital Prana with the Samana as well as Apana Prana at the navel center. By the mutual impact of these Pranas, one set of Pranas moving downwards and another set of Pranas moving upwards, create a new Prana that is named as Udana Prana. This newly generated Prana by the impact of four existing Pranas is basically a life force and the spiritual energy. By the yoga Sadhana this Udana Prana is brought to Muladhara charka by natural process and by the heat/energy of Udana Prana it piers the Muladhara, and from there it is allowed to ascend by yoga practices and gradually this passes through Swadhisthanam and Manipura chakras before it reaches to the Dhahara chakra, the heart center. At Dhahara chakra, it penetrates either on Rama Dwar/gate or Arama Dwar/gate or at the Ichha Dwar/gate. If it strikes at Rama gate, spiritual aspirant gets the feeling of happiness. It's penetrating at Arama gate gives the dual feeling of happiness and sadness because of the problems/miseries on the horizontal plane. If life force at Dhahara chakra strikes at Ichha Dwar/gate, then an aspirant feels the state of Apoor Bhava. It is the blissful state at Dhahara chakra. And if life force penetrates correctly at the Ichha gate, it can ascend with high kinetic energy and easily reaches to Apex center on passing through Visuddhi chakra, Lambika chakra and Ajna chakra. At Dhahara, life force gives Nada of Hreem and Aum automatically. If life force penetrates at Rama or Aroma gate, the chances for reaching the Apex state is remote. This may happen because of the lack of getting magnetic functional energy from the Dhahara chakra into the life force, which may not be adequate to reach the highest center easily.

In general, Udana Prana increases the spiritual energy in Sadhaka and by its help when it crosses the Dhahara through Ichha gate/Nadi; it takes with it the Soul to the Ajna chakra. After ascending, it gets purified at Visuddhi and Lambika chakras. Sadhaka can himself understand easily from which location of Dhahara chakra, the life force has penetrated to Ajna chakra. Infact Udana Prana/ life force is the carrier of the Soul to sky. It is sky ness carrier with divine and Godly energy. Each one of us has this energy, but it is required to be generated, directed, felt, worshipped and finally to be taken along with the Kundalini power and Soul to the abode of silence converting it into the light at the Ajna chakra.

There are other sub Pranas named as Naga, Karma, Kurkrara, Devdata (Vayu) and Dhananjeya. These are basically required to carry out the reflex functions of the body like eyes closing/opening; removing the Vayu/air from the digestive system by Dakara etc.; and vomiting function when system needs to vomit etc. Out of these sub Pranas Dhananjeya Prana is very significant. By this Prana, which is trapped in the abdomen region, the dead body of a person gets swelling and bolted up. Before pyres is lid or before cremation, keeping the body on the ground, the breath trapped in the abdomen is released by lower organs by the impact of handling the dead body and thus Dhananjeya Prana leaves the dead body. It is generally last to release from the body. Some times, if it is not released through lower organs and instead it ascend to lungs and heart, the dead body gets the consciousness even on the burial ground and even before the pyres are lid. These are rare cases but happen practically and also have been reported and duly documented. This is all by the miracles of Dhananjeya Prana. Basically Dhananjeya Prana is earth bound and Udana Prana is sky bound. Both are in the Udana/navel center/stomach. Dhananjeya Prana may act after death where as Udana Prana is made to act in the living body to uplift him and makes him divine/ spiritual. Basically Prana is generated from breath, but it is on much higher plane/level with much higher energy than breath. For dead body Prana mixes with food and get trapped in stomach with the partially digested/ undigested food and this acts as Dhananjeya Prana after the death of a person, and at times even at burier grounds its presence is felt. This shows that food needs Prana for digestion and it has the capacity to hold the Prana even after death.

After death the Prana leaves either through eyes, nose, mouth or ears. It all depends where are the inclination of Vasanas/desires exist in the mind at the time of death. If a person wants to smell a particular odour at the death bed, his Prana may leave through nose. If he wants to hear melody, etc, it may leave through ears. Similarly if he is very much desirous to see or eat some thing, then his Prana may leave through eyes or through the mouth, respectively. But if an advance spiritual aspirant is able to bring his Prana up to the Ajna chakra then it is certain that his Prana will leave only through the Apex center and from no where else it can leave the body. For yogis, Prana leave as light through the Apex center and merge with the supernal light. Leaving of Prana depends on thoughts at the time of death. Some Prana is always trapped as Dhanjaya Prana in the abdomen and leaves through lowest centers only. This may happen sometimes after the death or at the time of death.

Beside above there is a Shastra known as Chhaya/image shastra. By the help of Chhaya/image, one can predict at least six months before when the person is likely to leave this world. For spiritually advanced Self-realized yogis, there is no Chhaya/image of their physical bodies when they are under the sun; they are transformed as full of light by yoga practices; however, just appear in the physical bodies/forms.

In short, type of Pranas, their importance, functions have been highlighted: from which location Pranas leaves the body; and what are the conditions to leave the Pranas from the particular sense organs at the time of death. The highest achievement for a Sadhaka is when his Prana leaves from the Apex center after the death, and he knows when he is likely to leave the body. All this is by the grace and blessings of Almighty; this one can achieve not even after his best efforts and Sadhana.

14.2 Is it possible to increase Prana by simple relaxation technique? Are the yoga practices necessary to increase Prana Shakti for pursuing meditation?

For success in meditation and to achieve deep concentration, it is absolute necessity to control breath, and thought process must be checked. Thoughtless state must be achieved and mental activities should be dissolved. For this Udana Prana is required, which can be increased by Kriya yoga and breathing exercises. This finally leads to raise the Kundalini power through Sushumna Nadi that helps the Sadhaka for meditation and mergence with the Supernal. Relaxation technique helps to give rest to the human system, mind, and nervous system and releases the excessive store energy to the system, which takes the system to slumbering state; but any way it does not increase the Prana Shakti and Udana Prana in the system, which can help to awaken the Kundalini power. Relaxation as the primary exercise is very useful for smoothening and organizing the breath pattern that is helpful in Kriya yoga to enhance the Udana Prana easily in the system. Breath is conceit as the part of Maya. Total relaxation without the help of the breath is not possible, and it is not feasible even to an Avadhoota. Also, question does not arise for the ascendance of Prana just by relaxation. However, it is helpful for body, mind and senses to be in relative-composed state, and without conflicting energy to disturb him during relaxation.

In the spiritual path of evolution there are five basic transit location namely Akara, yakara, Arthchandra, Arohi, and Bindu, which give/transmit to Jeeva: Rupa; Nama; Bhakti; Priyam; and Asti; respectively. These physical astral virtues and their representations are the effect of the cause of ascendance in the path of the unknown, particularly Rupa/figure and Nama are beyond Maya-illusion as the divine beauty. By simple relaxation one cannot achieve these virtues; and even the glimpse of these priceless decors in the human life.

Furthermore, it may be noted that Eshwara, Gayatri and Brahma has five faces. They are known as Panch/five Brahmas. Lord Shiva removed one of the head of Brahma because of his false egoism and un-mirthful claim. Although Brahma is the creator, still there are no temples (a very few) for the worship of Brahma on this earth. Only Vishnu and Shiva are mostly worshipped being the God of Satto Gunna and Tammo Gunna, respectively; and have maximum temples for their worship. Brahma, the creator, the God of Rajo Gunna is hardly worshipped.

King and Grahastha/family men are never relaxed because of various responsibilities and activities of kingdom and their families, respectively. Their time is not theirs. They hardly spare time to be with the Self and relax. On the contrary, a beggar is reltively more relaxed most of time, and not even much bothered for his future. If he gets something, he is happy and even if he does not get, he feels relaxed. He is totally surrendered to the God for his welfare. His time is of his own and he prays, sings the song praising God and feels totally relaxed within himself, and is unaware of his surroundings and comforts. He is truly in ecstasy. If such a high order of non-awareness and relaxation prevails for the Sadhaka then he does not need yoga practices for pursuing meditation. Being relaxed, he is in meditation and with the Almighty.

In short, high level of mental and physical relaxation and unawareness is a stage of Samadhi. Under these conditions, spiritual aspirant does not need practices of yoga. By deeper relaxation in unawareness, detachment, and without any prejudices, he is in the state above that of Turiya when he is totally merged in the devotional songs of his lord without any formal yoga practices. Otherwise mergence with the Supernal with just temporary relaxation is a hypothesis and may be true hypothetically and not other wise with a practical viewpoint.

14.3 Why most of the people are scared for the vertical travel to take the higher spiritual path for the Self-enlightenment?

The path of Self-enlightenment is the most difficult path on this earth. It is the skyward path. For the skyward journey one needs to leave most of the horizontal accessories and activities, and it is not possible for every body to leave the material goods and worldly comforts. The world is Maya and it has all the attractions/gimmicks to attract the Jeeva to enjoy. The skyward path of Self-enlightenment is the path to be in the void; to be alone; and to be with the blessings of the Almighty. To achieve His blessings is not the mechanical process. One can achieve His blessings by His grace and only if He wants to bestow. Horizontal path has some hope and guarantee for achievement of the desired results/comforts; but vertical path is the probe in the darkness and there is no surety for any achievement and even for His grace. All depends on His mercy. One follows the divine path of Self-realization by the mercy and kindness of Almighty otherwise even the inclination to follow this path does not arise. Even if inclination is bestowed, the difficulties in the path leave no stone unturned to discourage the follower. So, most of the spiritual aspirants, even if they are interested, are scared to take up the vertical journey. They pray God outwardly by lighting lamp, put agarbati before God's idol and pray, do some pooja, Aarti etc and beg for material comforts.

Vertical path is full of difficulties; it is the path both with positive and negative inclinations. Any time one can fall/bent towards negative inclination and can suffer miserably. This path is the path having multiple anti-poles. Horizontal path is the path of awareness and full of mental activities. Mind is mutative and so the path is also variable depending on the horizontal norm. But, vertical path is a straight and narrow path without any change and glamour. It is dry and hard path. Horizontal path is governed by cause and effect. But in vertical path cause is Shiva and desire is Shakti. It is the process to couple Shiva and Shakti to cause evolution. There is no interaction that causes evolution in the horizontal path. In horizontal worldly path cause is Brahma and effect is Maya—the illusion.

On the contrary vertical path revolves around the cause of Shiva and effect of spiritual evolution. Both are anti-poles of the Maya, but Maya is also Brahma. So, horizontal and vertical paths are the two sides/corners of the Almighty as the anti-poles; and away from each other. Horizontal activities and worldly life of a human being are governed by manifested Brahma – Saguna Brahma; and the vertical activities are in the control of the absolute—the un-manifested; void; silence; and the achievement in the vertical travel is governed by Nirguna Brahma. Sada Shiva is the cause of manifestation from the absolute; the un-manifested void. Nada – AKSHAR BRAHMA governs the horizontal manifested world – the Maya; where as absolute silence is the domain of Sada Shiva – un-manifested void.

Desires creates feelings and to fulfill desires mind, Jeevatma, Brahma – the Maya, cooperate through the outer manifested world but if the desires are not fulfilled by influence of 'X' factors – the unknown cosmic forces, the individual becomes against the Jagat – the Brahma. If he is successful his egoism is boosted and he gives credit to the self and not to the Maya and not even to the X-factor that have really contributed to his success silently. In the same way Jagat/world is in between soul and Supernal and unless there is no cooperation of Maya i.e. the Jagat/world, the soul cannot merge with Supernal. So, Maya needs to be propitiated for any success even in spiritual vertical journey. Horizontally, the Maya is very powerful and only by His wish vertical journey can be undertaken. In other words unless and until a person does not develop Vairagya/detachment from the horizontal activities, he cannot proceed to the vertical path. So desires must be curtailed to take up spirituality. Man must be desire-less then only divine vertical path can be commenced. Similarly, Jeeva can only pray Eshvara/Almighty, provided Jagat/world—the Maya, cooperate with him. Until then he will be merged with Jagat— the world, and will be bounded in the horizontal moorings. When these moorings of Maya for the Jeeva is ceased to exist, then only he starts climbing the vertical path. In horizontal journey, the solution can be found for any activity. It is tangible journey but in vertical travel nothing can be proved and no solution can be easily apprehended.

Maya – Jagat puts lot of resistance to take the vertical journey. Aham/self of the individual comes in the way and miseries are put forward by Maya – the Jagat; these will pull the Sadhaka back to the horizontal plane even if the Sadhaka puts his best efforts to conquer it. So grace of the Maya – the collective worldly force – is very essential so that vertical journey can be commenced. Without blessings of Jagat – the world, a Sadhaka cannot proceed since being in physical form even for commencing spiritual vertical path he needs to depend on horizontal activities and various types of assistance from the world – the Maya. So Maya must allow a Sadhaka by his grace to leave him and it is not that easy the Maya shall cooperate to leave his own moorings. So to adopt the vertical path depends on the mercy of Maya – the Brahma that is the anti pole of Sada Siva – the un-manifested void – the peak of the verticality. That is the only reason why very courageous people by the grace of Almighty can take up vertical journey to the abode of Almighty. The Maya – the jagat needs to create favorable circumstances for such Sadhakas to take up the vertical travel. Grace of the world and co-operation of the worldly people are essential for vertical travel. Sadhaka needs to know/understand Jagat/Maya/ world very closely. He needs to dissolve his ego before/in the world. He must be humble. His ego must be flexible. All horizontal problems he must accept happily. He must accept defeat temporarily with all humility. He needs to pray 'X' factor, pray Maya, accept superiority of other worldly human beings. Withdrawal and defeat from Maya, Sadhaka must accept as the blessings to take up the vertical journey. He must be aware that this is a dualistic world. Nobody is always winner. Situation changes very rapidly. He must be clear that the possibility of defeat is opened up for the success with time. His ego must not interfere if he is defeated temporarily. Right adjustment and re-adjustment need to be carried out in the horizontal plane for taking upward journey. Time, space and consciousness are always mutative; a Sadhaka must be disciplined to know the depth of this philosophy for the skyward journey.

For self-strength a Sadhaka must practice Kumbhaka and use Shuniyaka techniques. Sadhaka must know that Vasudeva even prayed to donkeys for not to bray before taking out the child Krishna from the prison of king Kansa. He even prayed to river Yamuna for giving the way in her stream of water so that he could cross Yamuna to bring Yogamaya baby to hand over to Dewaki. For travel to the vertical path Sadhaka's ego must not come on his way. He must not show the egoism even to the donkeys. He must know that the world–the Maya is much more powerful than an individual. No single individual Sadhaka can fight with Almighty Maya in the horizontal plane since he survives on horizontal plane and takes journey abode to the vertical and again comes back to horizontal plane for his survival. So without co-operation of Maya – horizontal plane activities, his journey to the vertical will be a dream and full of miseries.

Sadhaka must know that he has duty for the known – the manifested world —the Maya and also for the unknown – the un-manifested world – the Sada Shiva – the void, and he cannot ignore any of them since both are bipolar of the same Almighty force – the Brahma. He must merge with unknown – the Ishwara, it is the spiritual realization and it is possible by vertical journey by merger of the Soul with Supernal by attending state of Samadhi. But to achieve this Jagat/world and Jeeva i.e.Maha Maya, the other half of Siva must be adored and must be understood prior to know its implication before taking upward journey. Horizontal travel gives photographic memory but does not induce the art of intuition where as vertical journey gives divine wisdom, intuition and divine qualities.

On the horizontal plane the dignitaries like Hitler, Alexander never accepted defeat and were not aware of the power of unknown 'X' factor; and because of their super ego and by not visualizing the superior power of Almighty, finally they got caught in the misery; they destroyed all their gains/moorings. Even Lord Krishna accepted the superiority of 'X' factor. He acknowledges that 'X' factor can defeat or help anybody. So in Mahabharat war he invited Karana, son of Kunti, through his mother Kunti so that Karna must fight on behalf of Pandavas since he was the son of Sun God. Karna declined but Lord Krishna accepted his supremacy and the power of 'X' factor. He also made it clear to Arjuna that Pandavas will win the war although their army is only of 6 Aksoni as compared to 12 Aksoni of Duryodana. The reason being the 'Dev Yoga' – the Krishna, as Dev Shakti, was with Pandavas.

So in the nutshell it can only be said that vertical path is the most complex and difficult path and by the grace of 'X' factor and by the blessing of 'Maya', and by the wish of Almighty, one can follow this path. By its own, no human being has courage even to think to adopt this path. One lives in horizontality and leads his life in horizontal activities. Vertical path takes us to source and horizontal path is the mundane path but without it cooperation, a Sadhaka cannot take up the vertical path.

Chapter 15

Meditation and Astral Body

15.1 Is it advisable to enter the stage of meditation through astral body?

Astral body is basically a Pranic cover on a human physical body. By practice, one can separate astral body from his physical body. Astral body is extremely light; it is like a windbag cover around a human body. This astral cover with full awareness can leave the physical body as if the Pranic astral jacket is flexibly covering the body. After being separated, astral body can go anywhere but it is closely linked with the gross physical body by the silver cord and connected with the navel center of the astral traveler. It takes all energy from the gross body through the navel center via silver Pranic cord. Astral body can travel in the sky; it can go to the far away places and get the varied information, which is passed to the consciousness of the gross body. After travel, astral body comes back and covers the gross body as if body was undressed for the time being, and has worn the astral Pranic cloths again. Gradually gross consciousness is back to the physical body as if body was in the dream state and remembered each and every aspect of the astral travel. But this astral travel does not add any spiritual wisdom and nor lifts the astral traveler by any mode to the higher plane of evolution. However, it is an achievement for an individual, being in gross body to know much about the other places, planes, people, and surroundings without being physically present there. It is indeed a miracle but without any addition to the spirituality and enlightenment for the self-evolution. However, it is closely linked with the Dhyana/meditation but with a different purpose and motives.

The astral body is made to release consciously from the physical gross body after years of specific practices. It is released when the Pranic force of the astral traveler is at the Ajna Chakra. The ways to release the astral body from the physical body for the astral travel require different techniques to be mastered that are beyond the scope of this book; and answer to this question cannot be dealt here.

After years of practice of yoga when the presence of Prana is easily felt in the Sushumna Nadi of the spinal cord, the whole biological system, particularly, vicinity of spinal cord is greatly magnetized with the spiritual/Pranic energy. Under such a stage of evolution, spiritual aspirant on concentrating his mental energies on astral plane can very clearly feel that the Udana Prana with Kundalini power are ascending upwards through astral body since astral body is very fine and closely linked with the physical body. Although the travel of Prana is through Sushumna but it may appear as if it is ascending through the astral plane. It can be felt mentally with the close awareness. This is because of the fact that astral plane is also magnetized by the spiritual force. This can even be felt by a sensitive person by touching the physical body of the spiritual aspirant just after the meditation/Dyana. The release of light through gross body and its Ojasav is through the astral body since it is a very fine and transparent cover on the physical body. This shines when Udana Prana is transformed into divine light and transmitted through this fine astral body.

Udana Prana after passing through various Chakras in the body; finally ascends upto the Ajna chakra and becomes the divine light. It is purified during ascendance at the Manipura, Dhahara, Visuddhi, and Lambika chakras. At Swadhisthanam, Udana Prana passes through heat of Agni/fire with moisture contents to evaporate gross earthly nano atoms and gets purified before it reaches to Manipura where it is further purified like a pure shining Mani/diamond; infact at Swadhisthanam Udana Prana is fully washed and made cleaned as this being water center. At Manipura after getting pure like diamond, it transmits AUM Nada. On ascending to Dhahara/ Anahata chakra, Udana Prana transmits honeybee type of Nada. Soul like an electron is ascended with Udana Prana from this location as the divine light. Thus, passing through Visuddhi and

Lambika, it is purified and finally pure Udana Prana rests at the Ajna chakra. In this way at the Ajna chakra Soul, Kundalini and Udana Prana are in perfect unison as the divine energy. After passing through awakening and dream states to the Sushupati state, the net quanta of all the ascended energies are transformed into astral energy; this transmits divine light gradually in steps. When Udana Prana/life force, Kundalini power and soul become bindu/ divine light point, it is called or termed as astral; here in this astral plane all types of energies get crystallized. After mergence of all energies at one single point, it is termed as astral energy point. Astral body is a separate identity; it is closest to the physical body; as a separate oneness astral energy/astral body, which can travel and can get separated from the physical gross body.

This astral body cannot merge with Supernal. It forms as a separate identity alone but along with the physical body and can transmit transformed radiance of spiritualism; however on getting separated from the physical gross body, it can have independent identity but cannot merge with Supernal. On the contrary, at Sahasrara on the travel path of light one can be in Turiya Tita state, where as Dhahara and Muladhara Chakras are locations/roots of light. These chakras absorb light that is descending from the cosmos via Sahasrara and Apex center downwards. But, an astral body is not the reservoir of light; it transmits light of the spiritual gross body. It remains separate but looks integral with the body. Moreover, it cannot be separated as it goes to sky as astral manicure Jeeva as light; it draws energy from physical body.

Astral activities and astral body are the part of Maya. It is fully aware of the travel undertaken. In Samadhi, one is not aware of astral body; it is non-awareness state. On the other hand, astral body can go 33 ft above the physical body, wanders and can come back. It is rather shunted back by the cosmic forces. It does not cultivate iota of spirituality in the aspirants/Sadhakas. One must not try for astral travel as a spiritual aspirant; however he can easily take up such journey by practice. Astral body is forced to leave sky by the cosmic forces as if astral body wants to take sky ness journey with wrong visa. Sky ness is the path of unawareness where as astral travel is with awareness and consciousness as an excursion to the sky. Astral body and its journey are Maya; it is in the Maya and with the Maya. Its travel is illusion and much away from Samadhi and mergence in the Supernal. Mergence in the void and sky ness journey is by the Almighty's grace. Astral travel is not allowed by the cosmic forces in sky, void and the Almighty. As human nose can detect the pleasant and foul smell; as tiger can reach the pray by smell; as dog can catch criminal by smell since his intuition is linked mostly with the nose and its capability to detect odor. So, the astral body travel is easily detected by the cosmic forces and is not allowed to go around because of impure and foul vibrations of the astral body. Furthermore, it is forced to return back immediately, by the unknown pressure of the cosmic divine forces.

In the light of the above meditator/Dhyani must transform by meditation his eyes and forehead very strong so that his eyes, ears and nose become TRIKAL VEDI—to penetrate in to beyond senses; and his aim must be to achieve universal consciousness, not limited to his gross body and mind. His consciousness must be extended to the sky ness and being in Samadhi, he must be with the omnipresent. On the contrary, astral travel is just the gimmicks before such an achievement even after years of long practices.

Spiritual aspirant by any norm must not concentrate on astral plane and astral travel. He must gather divine light, must nourish life force and concentrate it on one point. He must make his breath as Shiva to transmit divine light to the root/physical gross body. This may enlighten him with the cosmic consciousness. Bindu/light point from Ajna chakra must travel on higher centers without the self-consciousness/awareness as pointed divine light in unison on merging life force and soul in the divine light.

Dhahara chakra is the spiritual residence of soul. There are six chakras below Dhahara/Anahata including three unknown un-visible chakras below Muladhara and four chakras above Dhahara including Akul chakra that are filtration points to transform Udana Prana into the pure divine light to ascend further. Maya is the ego and its awareness must be dropped at all the chakras to reach the final stage of mergence and to be in the Samadhi. In meditation there is no awareness and no ignorance; and if awareness exists, this must be dropped at every stage.

Further it must be noted that on contrary to spiritual divinity, astral body is a light glowing worm where there is only twinkling of light, which is temporary and fades away with the disappearance of the worm. It is only illusion but it seems as if fundamentally it is light source. Astral body is just the fine body, retaining the shape of light. It is hallucination. It is Maya and deceiver to the spiritual aspirant.

In short, divine light is a cosmic light, and mergence with Supernal and Samadhi are the ultimate achievement of life. Astral travel, Dhyana through astral body travel do not lead the aspirant any where except in illusions without any spiritual evolution.

Chapter 16

Maya/Illusion and its Role

16.1 What are Maya and its role in spiritual evolution? How a Sadhaka/spiritual aspirant for his spiritual journey must deal with the Maya?

It is extremely difficult to understand, and define Maya – illusion. However, in simple words "M" of Maya can be taken as mystery, "A" of Maya as apparent, "Y" as yield, and last letter "A" of this can be manifested as arbitrary. So Maya can be defined as "A mystery that looks very apparent but yields only as arbitrary in its entire final outcome".

Udana Prana has been transformed by the impact and close interaction of various Pranas in the navel region. It has more of the sky contents than the earthly contents; it ascends through Sushumana Nadi through various charkas and reaches to Ajna chakra as a pure divine light. Entire physical system of an aspirant/ Sadhaka gets spiritually magnetized with the years of correct Kriya yoga practice. The ascent of the Udana Prana in the system takes place with awareness. The awareness of the ascent of Prana is Maya. In each Chakra, the awareness must be dissolved before the Udana Prana ascends to the next higher chakra. Gradually with practice, awareness turns to unawareness as learner /driver of a vehicle is very cautious initially and fully aware of, and later after learning he drives automatically without much awareness. As mother is emotionally and mentally immerged towards her baby with affection without awareness since awareness gets totally dissolved in baby's love; she becomes totally unaware and does not know how she loves her child. Similarly awareness of Sadhaka/spiritual aspirant gets immerged in unawareness after a long practice. Aspirant must propitiate Maya since Maya is all powerful and unless the Maya give the way, unawareness in the process of ascends is not feasible. Awareness acts in such a way as if the Sadhaka/ spiritual aspirant is taking milk in the dream. It looks as if he is in blissful state enjoying milk but there is no milk in the dream; it is all illusion/Maya. One can enjoy milk when he is in a wakeful state and really having the milk. It means one must be fully immerged in the activity and even unconscious thought of any kind must not disturb him then only he can enjoy bliss that he cannot describe. It is the confidence trick of Maya to create awareness to keep projecting a sense of separateness. It is the treachery of Maya that the awareness automatically pours in during ascent of the Udana Prana. It is nothing but illusion; Maya plays tricks of the biggest possible illusion as one wants to ascend from the horizontal path to the vertical path. Maya is the play of Shiva and Shaki in the horizontal plane. Maya acts as if it is playing a divine game. Awareness is projected as the cosmic energy and resists mergence of soul with the Supernal with a huge force. Shakti/power can project as Shiva since Shiva and Shakti are the dialectic possibilities of opposite poles.

Almighty/Ishwara has created Maya. Maya is the part of Brahman. This Srishti/world is the play of Maya and in other words, it is the game of Brahman. Both Brahman and Maya are the dialectically opposite poles of the same reality. This world is created by Brahma; Brahma is Maya; so Maya has to protect this Srishti/ world. Maya is the king of horizontal activities where as spirituality is the vertical ascent to merge with the Supernal. Both Maya and spirituality are dialectically opposite to each other. If Sadhaka takes the vertical journey, it is against Maya. He is rebellion for Maya, so Maya will put forward all the resistance in his path of vertical travel. Maya cannot tolerate vertical travel of Sadhaka, and it is against his nature to allow Sadhaka to leave his kingdom. Maya tries to put him back, misguides him since Maya is very powerful. Maya tries to hold back, demodulates the Sadhaka for the vertical journey, and considers the spiritual aspirant as rebellion of his regime. Maya creates all miseries for a Sadhaka in the horizontal plane. At times, he feels miserable.

The Ishwara has created Maya. Maya started his role from NONENESS to ONENESS to MANYNESS as the play of Brahman for his own pleasure/ happiness. The child is always unaware of his activities, being simple, Godly and merged fully with his play. Maya plays trick of awareness to misguide the child and thus attract him to the worldly activities by putting him in illusion.

In fact, Maya is not different from Ishwara. Maya is the base and it is manifested in many ways where as Ishwara being dialectically opposite to Maya is un-manifested, Poorna and fully filled with Satto Guna. He is unaware because of His un-manifested state and is away from all non-virtues. On the contrary, Maya is the combination of Sattva, Rajasava and Tamasava Gunas; it is formless oneness awareness and dialectically opposite to the un-manifested Ishwara being his own part. Maya is a living, charged manifested Shakti/power and it is a part of cosmic energy. Brahman as Maya is completely in aware state whereas Maya as Brahman is nearer to Ishwara and is in unaware state of existence. Dream state is the state of subtle Maya state where one thinks himself being in blissful state as being in the state of awareness but when he is awaken from dream state he finds himself nowhere near the bliss. From Kula to Akula Charkas, Sadhaka must shed awareness to ascend to Chida akasha other wise Maya being very powerful may drop him back from higher state of evolution.

There is no point to take the Udana Prana in hurry from lower to higher chakras. One must transcend each chakra from awareness to unawareness state. In Swathisthanam, the entire human past urges must be fulfilled. In Muladhara, instinctual desires must be comprehended/enjoyed/fulfilled. In Manipura, pure light like Mani must appear and in Dharara/Anahata Chakra, Prana must be illuminated with the soul light. Before the Ajna chakra, Mukhya/ Udana Prana must have been transformed into the divine light. Otherwise, Prana will only supply oxygen to the brain center without any spiritual evolution. Bio-spiritual atoms cannot gather at Ajna chakra if Mukhya/main Prana has not transformed fully into the divine light after crossing Visuddhi and Lambika Chakras. Turiya State must not have any Prana. If Prana exists in Turiya, this shows it is illusion of Turiya. Turiya is a semi-wakeful state.

In Akula chakra, all type of awareness must diminish. Sushupati State along with Turiya must be perfected before the light ascends further in Chida akasha.

It must be understood that Kundalini itself with three and half inch coils is in the state of Samadhi in Muladhara. A Sadhaka by spiritual practices can awaken this for higher evolution. Only at Manipura, Kundalini cools down and it can send Pranic energy to 72000 nerves before it is further ascended to Dhahara chakra. Without the grace of Almighty, no one gets absolute peace. One can be in like Samadhi but not in actual Samadhi without His blessings. When the microcosm itself becomes light after ascent of Udana Prana, then only one can enter Samadhi. This does not depend entirely only on Prana; it is His/Almighty wish and grace. Broadly, it can be said that yoga is Sandhya and meditation is Siddhi. Time, space and consciousness are continuum, and only Samadhi can take subtle ego away.

Nobody in this world is above Maya. Without propitiating Maya, one cannot make any progress in the vertical journey. Breathe is also Maya; by mercy of breath and its grace vertical journey can be taken up. Gyana/knowledge is helpful but without the mercy of Maya, no progress can be made in vertical journey. There are more chances of failure in spirituality than success since all vices of the horizontal world including Kama, Krodha, Greediness, Ahankara/ego, Mamta/attachment can any time deceive the Sadhaka and he can be thrown back in the mundane world again and again. With the mercy of Maya and grace of Almighty, one must observe silence in every breath to be with the spirit; chanting can be helpful to be in silence and to be in spirit.

In short, for spiritual evolution, a Sadhaka must look forward for the grace of Maya, Almighty, Guru and his own prayers and devotion; and finally the mercy of Supernal. However, still there is no surety of any kind without His/Almighty own blessings. These techniques and means are futile if He, the Almighty, does not want to open His own gates.

16.2 How a sadhaka/spiritual aspirant can conceive and understand the role and scope of Maya/illusion in this mundane world?

To conceive Maya, to understand it, and to explain its role is itself a Maya/illusion. The complexity exists in it self, because it is illusion, it is Maya. The complexity is that Maya/illusion needs to be explained by Maya/illusion only so it is very complex to express and difficult to grasp it.

The Maya is manifested Brahma; Brahma is Maya. Un-manifested Ishwara has created Maya as the manifested duality for His own play. Maya is the Leela/play of Ishwara, and it is mutative identity. It is it self a separate awareness. This awareness creates all doubts and Maya confuses snake with rope and vice versa. Maya is a center less center and it revolves around it self, which is again center less center. It creates dilemma of separate ness. Maya is center less center as visible but it is not traceable. That is what the illusion/Maya is. Maya creates Aham; I- ness. The feeling of other ness than the self is Maya. Maya is not the cause of creation. Maya is separate identity as the effect of creation. Absolute is all alone. To break its monotony, absolute – the un-manifested Brahma has created Maya – the manifested identity, which has created many-ness as the image of the un-manifested Absolute with its power of manifestation to create the cosmos with the living beings/Jeevas. The creation, sustenance, manifestation and dissolution are as per this Absolute's own desire to enjoy and play through the Maya/illusion – the manifested Brahma. Out of Absolute's own attributes, Maya has been created as duality as the awareness of the Absolute. However, fundamental Absolute is beyond awareness. Otherness as the creation by Absolute is Maya, which is the cause of the birth of many- ness as its manifestation and multiplying desires.

In the time memorial it was Ishwara, the Absolute; and in its one fourth reflected Bindu/point by the first throbbing in the center less center, the relative cosmos was created that is the part of Absolute – Absolute. The Brahma, the creator, being from the main source of the Absolute – Absolute; it contains Shiva-Shakti. The vibration/throbbing due to the unknown reasons in the cosmos divided Shiva and Shakti. Furthermore, the breath of Ishwara may create absolute – Absolute. The Absolute by His will create non-Absolute – the Maya/manifested cosmos. Thus, in the manifested cosmos, the number of skies was created/appeared by the divine mystery and in the sixth sky the birth of atom took place that created the mysterious continuation of the world and living beings. By filtering through the space in time memorial, the atomic control developed the communication through Shabda/Nada. Thus, the birth of Shabda formed Bindu/point in the relative sky in the cosmos. By Spanda and Pratispanda of the Bindus/points in the relative sky of the relative cosmos the awareness appears. The awareness is the super power and the part of Absolute Brahma that transformed into Shakti/power that is the Maya/manifested power of Brahma with the name and form. By its awareness it is simultaneously away from the awareness of Brahma since it is dualistic; it is being manifested as a part of Brahma. In Maya, as well, creative omnipresent power of Brahma prevails. However, Para Shakti/power of the Absolute, forgetting its basic reality, takes care of the cosmos both in limited and unlimited way, as and when it is required, even during the time of crisis in the hands of Maya.

Maya is finite in the ocean of infinite but it is very powerful in this manifested world. Maya is forgetful of Absolute. Under the influence of Maya, one considers him self egoistic with full power and does not care of the God's grace. Only in Samadhi, awareness of the self is withdrawn and Maya gets fully merged into Brahma. Samadhi is always without awareness and it is the Brahmi Sthithi/state. In Samadhi, Maya withdraws in totality or gets fully merged with the un-manifested Brahma and becomes the part of Absolute.

Guyana/knowledge is the greatest deception to the Sadhaka. It can take the spiritual aspirant to the state of KAIVLYA as if he is the only preceptor of the Absolute. Dhyana is the part of Guyana with awareness and it is in the purview of Maya until Laya/mergence, when the total withdrawal of consciousness is attained by itself. It is the state of Samadhi, the mergence, without awareness. No Maya/illusion exists in this state. It is the state of original child-like innocence. In this state there is nothing to listen and nothing to worship. It is the state of total withdrawal; and in this state,

Maya in the name of God, is merged in Almighty without any awareness/consciousness. The Kriya; the action; the subtle conscious, the gross feeling etc; every thing related to Maya/illusion are merged in the Absolute in this state of Laya, the mergence.

Maya is not the enemy of human being and nor it is the best friend. Maya in relation to Brahma is real and one and the same, being the undivided. Brahma and Maya apparently look two different identities. But both are same one being un-manifested Brahma and the other one being manifested (Maya). Memory, to call back, is the trick of Maya; it is just to hold back the Sadhaka from the spiritual progress. When He/Almighty recalls, no memory and nothing remain; it is void; it is the un-manifested state of the Absolute. Maya gives the way to reach the state of Parashuniya – the Absolute.

Without the grace of Maya, it is not feasible to take up vertical path to the Absolute. We need to pray and regard the Maya. No Mantra, Yantra and Tantra are helpful if Maya does not withdraw its subtle memories; Vidya/knowledge; Avidya/ignorance; action/reaction; work etc. All these are the part of Maya in the absolute terms. Thinking is Para Maya; through Maya one can ascend, and reach to the state of STITHA PRAGNYA, which is Avidya/ignorance. All varieties and kind of things are basically a part of Maya but MOUNA/Absolute silence is withdrawal from Maya. It is the greatest enlightenment. Awareness is lost in enlightenment. Cause and effect are made senseless, purposeless in the state of enlightenment. Mind is fully vacated in the state of enlightenment; it is then void all around. The state of void is the state of Absolute silence without any awareness.

In short, Maya/illusion plays a game of disruptions and uses the art of skillful disruption for a Sadhaka when he prepares himself to go higher up in the path of spirituality to take up the vertical journey. Basically Maya/illusion is the internal disruption of Ishwara as the resistance by the Ishwara for the mergence of the soul with the Supernal. This disruption is to be controlled by and through Maya by the grace of Ishwara to follow the higher path of spirituality to be with the Ishwara/Absolute.

Chapter 17

Silence and its Significance

17.1 What is silence? How one can achieve silence to be peaceful and happy?

Silence is an integral state and the most peaceful state of a Sadhaka/spiritual aspirant. The silence is basically wordless, thoughtless, mindless, and breathless state. On negation of breath, suspension of breath, mind is negated and silence appears. In presence of breath, varieties of thoughts are sprouted and silence is withdrawn from the mental plane. Silence is not wordless-ness; just keeping quiet is not silence. To observe Mouna/keeping quiet is a primitive silence, it is outwardly silence. Absolute silence prevails when one is within the self and soul is merged in the Supernal. Other modes/types of silence are just the relative silence. One can easily communicate in relative silence when the receiver is also in silence. The higher level of relative silence can produce ideas, and it can receive the thoughts/signals. In silence one can dream. Dream state is also a type of silence state. Basically mouth is shut but all the senses are in working state and senses are opened to receive thoughts from sub conscious mind. A mute picture goes on in the mind. It is a state of relative and a temporary silence state.

The suspension of consciousness and sub conscious states only lead to the higher state of silence. It is only possible when one enters from dreamy to Sushupati/deep slum state to Turiya/ transcendent state when mind has been negated and breath is partially suspended. In general, in the silence state all the Karma Indriyas, Guyan Indriyas and Tanmantras are made functionless. It is possible with Shuniyaka, and the state of suspension of breath is achieved. When all the Indriyas/senses are function less then mind does not react because it does not get energy since breath is suspended, and so the higher degree of relative silence prevails. In this state, there is no provocation and no objective-subjective, and nor subjective–objective reactions of the mind. There is not action – reaction in the mind; and nor any subjective or objective motivation operates in the mind. It is the silence – a higher degree of relative silence. But as soon as consciousness with awareness with outside memory enters, the silence is disturbed. Also, it can be disturbed by inside sub consciousness thoughts. Any mutative horizontal breath disturbs the equilibrium of silence. Breath has multiple complex vibration pattern of external world and it disturbs the silence to the major extent by the multiplicity of conscious thoughts. This may lead to propagate and create the various desires that can ruin/disturb the inner developed silence partially/ completely.

Basically absolute silence prevails only in the state of Samadhi and in the Turiya tita states. In other states one gets only the semi-silence. By alertness, being consciousness, one can prolong relative/ semi silence by yoga practices. However, a simple breath can change the scenario of spiritual feeling and non-sense mundane feeling can pour in mind resulting in disturbing the silence achieved. One must understand that silence is mutative. No one can be in silence for a long duration by conscious and semi-conscious efforts. However, these are the only means to be in relative silence.

Ego in the consciousness can appear by Maya/illusion that brings various desires. Desires invite pleasure memories, which give rise to grow other series of desires that subsequently attack the silence very violently. This leads to change the thoughts, affects the mind, provocates the mind leading to suffering both subjectively and objectively by spoiling the silence completely. On the contrary real relative silence with consciousness when nullified by Turiya/ transcendace state brings absolute partial silence. This state of silence continues till the soul light prevails and increases. This state of unconsciousness/unawareness under the umbrella of soul light gives the bliss of absolute silence and happiness. Soul light is above any mutation and hence it gives real silence, the state less state of the Absolute.

Jeeva is I ness; and Jeeva, accompanying the soul as Jeevatma. It affects the sanity of soul; its true divine light; and hence the absolute silence cannot prevail in the presence of Jeeva. Therefore, desire-less attitude and rebellious attitude cannot be silenced/ controlled in presence of Jeeva. The silence can only be partially established if Indriyas/senses are properly trained to behave like a soul, which is non-mutative; so as the desires of Jeeva are temporarily dissolved. In other words one must be JITENDRYA – the winner of the dynamic desires of the senses/Indriyas to be in silence without getting provoked by any gimmick of the senses. One needs to propitiate the breath, so as to negate it by its own mercy to merge into the silence. Sadhaka must learn the art to be PAWANJAYA—winner of breathe; and he must be able to command the breath. Existence of breath shall be in his control to be in the zone of silence. The silence is the super commander but it can be destroyed by any horizontal urge very easily. Alertness is to be strictly observed to prolong the silence state. There must not be any reaction because of any type of the horizontal disturbances; one should be ROCK LIKE SILENCE. It is only possible when aspirant is above the limitation of consciousness. Any type of consciousness in the horizontal plane including sub consciousness must not disturb the silence. All subjective and objective symptoms of any kind to be nullified and must be shed down. Shuniyaka and breath suspension are the most effective techniques to invite the silence. However, any horizontal breath can spoil the silence any moment. The silence zone is very delicate and very critical zone. Prolonging/elongation of the silence in the human life are really very difficult tasks like Kukukshetra Sangarama/war. It is extremely difficult to increase the period of silence. It is just like to arrest the wind without solid boundaries.

Silence cannot be achieved by physical and mental efforts. If by active conscious efforts, the silence is tried, then there are chances that one suffers in sub conscious state; and many disturbances are surfaced again and again on the conscious level from the sub conscious state. Any sub conscious feelings always try to disturb the silence with full vigor. So the memory of the sub conscious should be avoided by using Shuniyaka/void methods. However, it is very difficult to control the higher forces of microcosm and macrocosm and avoid them to react so as to maintain the achieved silence. One could only forcefully and consciously try such that sub conscious thoughts must not make the unknown linkages to disturb the silence. Even reacting and answering the conflicting issues might disturb the achieved silence. Some times one has to keep artificial outer behavior to avoid the conflicts but inside poison of disturbances may churn more violently to create an era to destroy the inner silence. However, one must always try to get fake silence inwardly if the external conflicts are severe and beyond control; but it will be far way from the real inner silence.

To live in the society one has to become outwardly CIVIC by keeping/observing the fake inward and outward culture of silence. However, for a long time such action and reaction of the outward conflicts cannot be avoided easily. There are very mutative. By ocean of inbuilt inner silence and philosophical inward inclination, this can be made possible. To keep silence one must act subjectively but objectively one must not react. To be silent one needs to learn this art of being INACT. It basically requires separating the inner world from the outer world; this is the only judicial way to be inwardly silent. Tide and waves of disturbances of outer world must be kept on the surface and inwardly one must be silent and calm like an ocean. This is the art of enactment to make the fortress of inward silence. INACTMENT is only feasible by having complete command on breath; by being consciously alert; and by controlling one's own emotions and reactions etc.

Enactment way of control to keep silence is not easily possible for one's own kith and kin. If one is disturbed inwardly in sub consciousness then his outward silence positively gets affected. The only way is to shield sub consciousness by all possible means and conquer over rebellious thoughts of actions/reactions to preserve silence. However, even for a highly spiritual advanced Sadhaka, it is not easily possible when one's own nearest are involved. By controlling the self/own outward reactions, the inward silence is likely to be positively disturbed. But for a common worldly man with his outward reactions, the sub consciousness is not affected since he lacks sensitivity being unrefined. But spiritual aspirant at times affects his mental and physical health by keeping MUTE WORD LESSNESS AND OCIFEROUS SILENCE till he clears his sub consciousness by rebellion thoughts. This is because the spirituality does not teach reactions and allows only actions, and at the same time makes a person highly sensitive. So in any active horizontal self-evolved problem/issue, a Sadhaka suffers to the greatest extent but for a common worldly man this is just a normal suffering. This is because of suppressing of natural feeling of reactions to keep the outward silence. Its reaction to the inward personality is enormous and highly critical.

In short, relative silence is mutative. To be in silence, the reaction of the self must be much less from a Sadhaka due to his capacity of tolerance. However, inwardly he gets disturbed because of the involvement in horizontal activities even if he follows the path of INACTMENT.

The absolute silence can only be achieved in Samadhi. In all other states and controls one gets mutative relative silence. This is only semi-silence. For horizontal life even this is an asset to live in peace.

17.2 How the silence is governed? What are factors that influence silence of human mind?

Silence is Maya/illusion. Maya is arbitrary, mutative and so the silence is never permanent. It changes with time, space and causation. Maya is awareness and so the relative silence is awareness. Being aware and fully vigilant one can save him self to fall down from the state of relative mental silence. However, absolute silence is the act of super consciousness.

This world is Maya/illusion so its negation is also Maya/illusion. Suppression of consciousness of reaction is Maya as well. It can sprout out of mind from time to time. Maya is Shakti/energy, and it can ascend vertically upwards. It is a Kriya Shakti and this is not different from source light. It is awareness and also a part of Brahma. Its dialectic possibility is Brahma. Maya is very merciful; it is graceful; one must worship Maya then only it may give way for the transcendental journey to merge with the Supernal. By its grace only one can cross the barrier of relative silence/awareness to be in the absolute silence/non-awareness; it helps to come/arrive to the doorstep of Samadhi. It is basically to ascend from Para-Apara level to Para-Para level of silence i.e. from the conscious silence that is with efforts to the silence without awareness and without efforts. If it is achieved then it is called Sahaj silence, which is nothing but the absolute silence. It is the stage of mergence of soul with the Supernal.

The Para – Apara silence, being at the state of awareness, controls the memories of the sub conscious state that creates the sufferings in the relative silence. This silence has to work against memories and make the aspirant/Sadhaka to suffer much more than experiencing the actual happenings of miseries. A memory of the sub conscious state is the worst. However, deep sleep is very helpful to forget such memories to ascend to the zone of silence. Sleep without dream is the best for the complete relaxation and to be in silence without memories. Silence is the rest of mind however conscious silence is illusion/Maya. Rest of the mind is basically out of any action and reaction even if the mind is awake. Such state of mind is wakeful rest. Observations of fresh breathe to enter and used breath to escape is the wakeful rest of the mind. This is

Maya since it is wakeful and conscious activity with awareness; also, rest of the mind even without action/reaction under these conditions is Maya i.e. the relative silence. Any moment it can be disturbed. Even a single ferocious breath can completely destroy the silence.

Maya – the relative silence cannot take the spiritual aspirant to the stage of Samadhi. Even in Turiya/transcendental state is partially illusion/Maya. And the divine light is Maha – Maya; it is much beyond the senses to conceive. Maha-Maya is mother and by her grace the divine path becomes approachable. It is Para – Para Shakti. It is Tirupura Sundari. All of us beg for her blessings for success in the spiritual path. One can only put his efforts, but granting grace is her prerogative and mercy. Maha – Maya is an active part of Almighty and only through this, silence can be achieved by following the vertical path and finally to reach un-manifested stage / Godly stage to be in absolute silence in the stage of Samadhi. One need not brood more on the past and try his best to forget past to come over sub conscious state and then over come conscious state to finally land in the super conscious state of perfect silence.

If one does not learn to be silent in his life, he is bound to suffer particularly in old age when even kith and kin will not listen and follow even his positive advice. Earlier one learns how to be silent, the better it is for positive and prospective living. The other inner meaning of silence can be taken as detachment. If one does not feel concern, he remains silent; and in other words, it can be said that he is not attached; he is fully detached. By Mantra chanting, the inner silence can be enhanced. Silence is the power of God; one must be silent to be with the Almighty. Generally, worldly people lose silence in views of the various problems being experienced by their kith and kin. However, it must be remembered/ known that kith and kin have their own Prarabdha. We are just the instruments for their birth to bring them in this world. Furthermore, silence is taught and understood by the subjective attitude; by physiological way of understanding the net situation. By objective means silence cannot be cultivated. Our soul, being un-manifested subjective dormant light is the institution of silence within us. It helps in silencing the mind, which in turn is the source and guide to put full stop for the wondering of senses unduly for worldly issues/problems.

Consciousness is a very powerful instrument to maintain silence by self-efforts. Para silence in the hands of Turiya; Maha -Maya can grace silence both in vertical and horizontal journey of life. Sita, the life force meets Rama, in the Chida akasha through the Setu/bridge of Sushumna provided by Maya through conscious awareness of relative silence. Hanuman the embodiment of silence did show humility even being capable of bringing SANJIVANI with in few hours; he did not act until Rama instructed him to bring for LAKSHAMANA when he was unconscious. Silence is manifestation of capability and humility; and one must not misunderstand it even in worldly dealings. Even Ravana observed the power of silence during war with Rama, and instructed his own Vaidya/doctor to attend Lakshamana when he was unconscious. Ravana understood that this war is the Dharmayudha/religious war, so by the power of his mental silence and without irritation followed the ethics of the war. This is all because of inner silence that guided him in the moments of crisis. Being internally in the state of absolute silence, he knew Rama – the Avatar of Vishnu – the God; and wanted to be killed by him in the war.

In short silence always gives positive results when you are not egoistic but silent. Agitated/disturbed breath can spoil the cultivated/developed silence. Yoga can evolve energy but cannot bring silence. Subtle ego developed out of Guyana/knowledge is much more dangerous than the gross ego and can disrupt the silence within no time. Even great Rishis like Narada have failed because of the subtle ego, which lead him to confront with Narayana—the God. In Maya/illusion, consciously one considers rope as snake; but when enlightenment approaches; ignorance disappears; even unconsciously one finds that rope is not a snake and vice versa. The best and the safest path to achieve silence is to be with the God; surrender to Him; to come to SHARNA GATI to Him as a child; feel carefree and safest as a child with the mother. Mother takes full care in all respects and keeps the child comfortable. Surrender brings PARA MOUNA – the absolute silence. Death is the mode of permanent silence; however suspension of breath is the path of silence. To be conscious of silence is the relative silence. SADA SHIVA; the mergence of Shiva and Shakti; soul and Supernal; and the Samadhi; is the absolute silence. And it is easily possible if the life force penetrates Ichha Nadi/gate at Dhahara chakra, then it passes through APOORNA BHAV NADI that leads easily to Supernal; mergence; Samadhi; and state of absolute silence.

Thus, it is seen that various factors govern the silence; and all are in the hands of Almighty since ABODE OF SILENCE is the God himself.

Chapter 18

Life Beyond Death

(A) 18.1 What is the Mystery of Life Beyond Death?

"Life beyond Death" is a chronological enquiry of different spiritual aspirants from the time memorial. This is a very mysterious question and this interests to each one of us very deeply. However, answers to such questions are never satisfying and one moves round and round and tries to seek their answers in different dimensions to satisfy the inborn curiosity. From birth onwards life is manifested; and death is an event, which extinguishes life; name and form of an individual; as soon as body becomes breathless. After the death occurs nothing remains; Jeevatma/soul becomes the part of the un-manifested regime; and a physical body gets dissolved in five basic elements, it is composed of.

Prior to know the death one must understand life because before death there was life. So the death is the continuation of life in other dimensions with different regime. As soon as the life manifests from the birth, it travels with name and form. Our birth is the effect of our parents but from where we have come before we born, is the cause. Before we are born, we were the part of un-manifested regime without form and name as light/soul. The same exists after death when we become the part of the un-manifested regime again. In between the two un-manifested regimes there is a manifestation of life with name and form for certain period where we exist and try to gain knowledge of life beyond death along with other mysteries.

Life is the linkage with infinite manifestation of the God, and death is the linkage with infinite mother of the soul. The mysterious secret beyond life is the spirit that enters as our soul when the life starts manifesting as the effect of the universal cause through the media of the couple - the parents. Life is originated from the un-manifested universe so life is both Chaitanya – the consciousness; and Jadah-the static; this is being the dualistic possibilities. So being in the physical form, one needs to worship both manifested and un-manifested Brahman i.e. both Maya/illusion and the Almighty.

The body/form exists so for soul remains in it. It means that life revolves around soul and soul is the light from the unknown. It is dielectrically opposite to the materials-the physical beings. Thus, it is absolutely essential to know the mystery of soul to know the secret of life, secret of death and life beyond death. The secret of soul can only be realized in Samadhi. No one can know the mystery of soul unless he merges in the Supernal. So without entering into the Nirvikalpa Samadhi, the secret of soul, the mystery of life and death will remain only an unresolved puzzle without any convincing solution. The further dilemma is, moment one knows this mystery, then soul does not want to stay in the body/form. Soul refuses to get identified. Unknown part of the soul cannot be known; and if it is known; it cannot be communicated. Hence this mystery remains mystery before the world. Only subject knows it as Anubhuti and one, and only that one knows who establishes himself with the Supernal being in Nirvikalpa Samadhi, but refuses to discuss the mystery, as it cannot be expressed in words. It is beyond expression so remains dormant from the time memorials. Knowing this mystery, soul cannot remain in the mortal world and leaves the form by His wish.

Life co-existence is a mystery with the cause of the universe and it exists between mixed and apparent truth. The illusion of life is the gap between these truths and this is filled with the cognitive knowledge. This is itself a Maya/illusion. The further dilemma to this is that mind thinks illusion as realization and realization as illusion.

The world exists with the fundamental ignorance. The manifested reality in the world is just transitory. This is bound by time, space and causation; it is transitory; it disappears as illusion.

The one that is the soul; remains as the permanent identity; the replica/ image of God, which is above illusion/Maya. Esteem soul is beyond death and it is unaware of transitory knowledge/nature. Death takes out all elements of the body: breath is suspended during death; senses lose their energy; heart stops; all major organs become dysfunctional at the time of death; and soul leaves the body. Under these conditions only coegulitive knowledge of the mind remains/ exists and soul remains just in the background. Soul is the deity/ idol of the body temple. We, the ignorant being only conduct the rituals in the temple, but never go to the soul deity residing in the body/temple that illuminates the complete system and makes it functional. This idol, the soul, is the power of eternity in us. It is the source of fundamental knowledge. Human being exhibits fundamental ignorance; revolves around birth; death; and considers illusion-the Maya, as the reality.

One revolves around Jeeva; self and mind; considering all these as the cause of creation. This is the fundamental ignorance of the human being. Self/ego is a false light. Jeeva does not give knowledge. This ignorance is itself AVIDYA/AGNYANA. However, both Guyana/knowledge and Agnyana/ignorance are closely related. Agnyana is a relative ignorance; and Guyana/ knowledge does not give realization. By this worldly/mundane knowledge one cannot reach God. Only by silence which is the abode of God, can give real knowledge and can bring us near to Almighty. Only silence can lessen the burden of ignorance. Death is the world of silence that is un-manifested, the abode of Spirit.

Life is the full of ignorance. Some total of knowledge of this world is like having squint eyes; and ignorance is like having blind eyes. One is needed to charge his spirit and required to go beyond every mundane thing. Journey to sky-ness that is to be in the abode of silence, as well surrender of mind and egoism, are the only paths to be with the Almighty. World does not allow us to approach silence by its worldly activities. AUM is the only symbol of silence and it is the holiest word; it is the manifestation of Supernal; and it is the symbol of fundamental silence.

By chanting SVADA AUM, one gets tranquility in 72000 Nadis and 73 crores (730 millions) of the body cells. AVADHA AUM gives the knowledge of silence before birth and after death. Linkage of the soul in this life is nothing but the linkage of silence being in this body. One must not be scare of death. Death is the natural corollary of the evolution. Life is the just like a bubble; its existence is transitory. It is not permanent. One can live maximum around 1000 months. In between birth and death i.e. in between two eternities, life is just a bubble; the manifested balloon. The one that cannot be known is permanent, is the soul. The purpose of life is to know, which we cannot see that is the permanent. To see/feel/visualize the permanence of life is the purpose of life; one can enter its premises to be with it.

The secret of life is eternity, to be with the un-manifest, the Almighty. To approach un-manifest, the soul light, through the manifest — the Maya/illusion is the sole purpose of our existence. Beyond form/body it is un-manifest, the abode of silence. The soul is not born, but entered our body and manifested it by five elements. The soul has occupied the premises of the body as light, as the part of un-manifest, the Almighty. To know this, to be with this, is the only purpose of life; and once it is known, the death and life beyond death will not remain a mystery.

(B) 18.2 Experience of Death in Life

Scientifically only by the process of elimination, we reach to the stage of unchanging permanent truth. In the same way, one finds that the soul is only permanent truth and reality that has existed before birth/ life, and will remain after death when life ceases to exist.

Soul has permanent relevance since it remains in the stage of Samadhi where as other significant and powerful physiological and psychological constituents of human form like mind, intellect, and ego do not exist and get dissolved before mergence. Life and death has no meaning for the soul since it can neither die and nor can take birth. Life and death cannot provide any answer for salvation, since salvation revolves around soul i.e. the mergence of soul with the Supernal. In the span of life, a common man does not get any glimpse of death as if there will not be the end of life and he will continue to live forever. Only the realized soul visualizes the end in every activity and feels/realizes that end/death will be the continuation of existence even after this life ceases to exist. The question of death bothers only to Jeevatma since it has to take re-birth to fulfill the worldly desires that has not been exhausted in this life. For soul there is no death; it is immortal as it was before the birth; and will remain unchanged after the death. Jeevatma carries memories of the past after death and looks forward to take birth for accomplishing and enjoying the sweet memories of the past life. Only enlightened souls become desire-less in the present life and for them death loses its significance since life without any cravings and desires is just like a death; and thus life and death both lose their importance. Life and death are the two sides of the same coin for them. In every breath, they are dying as well as re-appearing, and they know very clearly and intrinsically the mystery of death.

Atma/soul thinks about the Absolute, it gets absorbed into Absolute after getting relieved/separated as pure Atma/soul. On the contrary, Jeeva in more complex manner is involved in my-ness and loses its purity during existence. Jeevatma thinks of relative absolute. In the nutshell Atma/soul, Jeeva, mind, Pragyatma and Jeevatma are closely linked with highly complex manner among themselves; and it is very difficult to apprehend their individual role in this divine play of the Almighty. Soul is Absolute in Absolute where as Jeevatma acts through mind. For any tangible actions/ results, mind becomes Chaitanya/conscious and through consciousness, all actions/Kriyas are carried out. In other words actions desired by Jeevatma are planned by mind, and executed by Chaitanya/consciousness under the force of Kriya /action by the human ego. Soul is dormant and is covered by the various layers of Maya/illusions; thus it becomes relative absolute; and so its light is not projected through the Maya. For the soul light, there is no birth and no death. It approaches to the horizontal level to give life to the body/form, and take the skyward journey to be with the Supernal and come back to be with the body till the human life exists. Soul can play with life and death; however there is no death for the soul. Thus, for the self-realized person who is living with the Self/soul in the existing life, there is no death for him. Life and death both are the same for the Self-realized person. He can experience death very closely being alive, as he wants.

For a Sadhaka, being in a manifested state and alive in the body/ form, his evolution revolves around the desire for the un-manifested/death state, which is dialectically opposite to the living state; but after being Self-realized, this dialectically opposite state vanishes; then he can be in both the states, or can be in any state as he wishes. No life; no death; no manifested and un-manifested states; all are the same for him.

There is death only for the manifest identity, Jeeva, and Maya, but no death for the soul. For pure soul, there is no evolution and no travel is required. I-ness of the soul is Maya and soul when gets awareness of microcosm; it becomes part of the Maya/illusion. The soul coupled with awareness or entangled with Maya turns to be Jeevatma, and on the contrary, when Jeevatma loses awareness, it becomes pure soul. There is no life without awareness. It is a pivotal point for the understanding of life beyond death. Furthermore, if one loses awareness, he can experience death as life vanishes/disappears immediately. So, in Samadhi, awareness disappears that leads to timelessness, then only one is with the spirit and he experiences death in these few minutes. However, as soon as awareness re-appears, desirelessness vanishes, soul again is re-coupled with Jeeva and it comes under the control of Maya. Nevertheless, experience of unawareness/death remains in a very feeble way in the mind of the Jeeva.

Absolute - the pure soul has no desire of any kind. As soon as desires prevail/appear, the creation of the cosmos commences, the manifestation starts. For the Absolute, this universe is a play as the net effect of His desires by His own light, which is beyond time, space and causation. This creation is as per the supreme will of the Absolute. Hence, Maya, this creation, is not different from the source - the Absolute. Maya is the part of the supreme/Absolute. Relative thinking of the Almighty and His dynamism is through Maya. Maya is the source of His Absolute manifestation where as Almighty is the un-manifested Absolute. Manifestation starts from Bindu/point, the un-manifested source, and ends up in the same Bindu/point. The great seers could not unfold this mystery of the supreme. By His grace, only this mystery can be understood since both Maya and Absolute are by His grace only. In addition, both fulfillment and unfulfillment of all activities/desires are by His grace/will only.

Life is not just feeling, emotion, breathing, eating, enjoying, it is in essence the silence in all activities in the manifested form. One needs to enter silence to be with the intrinsic life. It is possible when the consciousness of the life is withdrawn and put back into the Dhahara chakra then only desires, feelings and manifestation of the mind disappear. When this is achieved, there remains no Ichha/desire, no Kriya/action, and no-dynamism and then only soul light manifests and ignorance created by the Maya is removed. This creates the silence of mind and its mergence with the soul light. This is the sole purpose of a human life. This Anubhuti can be experienced through silence and silence only. Practice of silence is the approach to the enlightenment and if it is achieved, the fear of death disappears.

When consciousness is resided in the Dhahara, then only the query rises in the mind of the spiritual aspirant: "Who Am I?" With time, beyond words in the silence, one understands the mystery of awareness and unawareness, as well as various reactions of the consciousness. This only reveals the mystery of silence that is beyond the human apprehension. One understands easily that silence is the food of the soul, and soul along with the source light can suck it. Subtle ego is trapped when silence is fully established. Only silence can face and stand before the Almighty, and can communicate with the soul. Silence is not just the suspension of the breath, but it is the consciousness engrossed with the pure soul. After such achievements in life, there remains no fear of death. In fact, Jeeva is scared of death and it has its subconscious desire to live in the astral body even after the death.

Now, it is very clear that what you are in the present life, the same remains after death. If Jeevatma is free from desires in this life, then only enlightenment prevails in this life and after death. Life is continuum even after death. Death releases soul as pure light/soul as existed in the active life. On the contrary, the release of Atma/soul as Jeevatma is equally feasible when Jeeva could not forget his past moorings during death, and dies with lot of unfulfilled desires and urges to fulfill all of them. Under these conditions, Atma is not free after the death and Jeevatma takes birth again to fulfill the un-accomplished desires. This is the sole cause of the re-birth of the Jeevatma. However, pure soul does not take re-birth; it merges in the Absolute, unless Almighty sends him to fulfill His purposes.

Some times Jeevatma is uplifted for the good and virtues actions done in the life span before death, to the level of pure soul, because of the mercy and grace of the Almighty. Such souls are sent back on the earth by the will of the God. A few Jeevatma perform rituals after death in Praloka and live happily there with the Devas. In due course they take much superior birth on earth based on their Karmas in the Pitraloka. A few Jeevatmas do penance in the Pitraloka to leave their desires, and repent for their wrong actions done in the life span before death. Such souls are allowed to live in Vasuloka and then promoted to live in Rudraloka, and exempted from the re-birth cycles but they do not get mergence with the Supernal. Some souls are sent to Aditya-loka by the Almighty/Absolute in due course to allow them to take birth as the prophets on earth, and this is as per His wish to fulfill purpose as desired and designed by Him..

Finally, in the nutshell, those who invite death of their own, they get total salvation. They follow Archidamarga and Dhumrajayamaga for salvation in their life span as per the ways and means given in Katho-Upanishad.

(C) 18.3 Death Within Life

To understand the concept of death is very mysterious and complex. Moreover it is more difficult to understand death within the span of life. If one can experience death in life then he will not have any fear of death. Then only he can live in death as he lives in life. For him death and life both are same. Experiencing death in life is the death of Maya - the illusion. He can raise himself above Maya if he feels/realizes/experiences death in life. Then only mystery of life and death will be clear to him while living. Feeling/realizing/experiencing death is nothing but the end of the cause of the cycles of his ego and Sankalpa. It means all his ego and Sankalpa will disappear and he will start living just for the sake of living as if he is mentally dead but physically alive. His experience of life and death are simultaneous. He lives without any desires, and so leaving the physical body/form is just a play for him since he lives without any attachment of any kind. Basically, he is very close to death being alive. Neither gimmicks of life attracts him and nor death creates any fear in his mind. For him there is no duality of life and death; he is very friendly and close to both. He loves death as he loves life. Death for him is just coming out from the close room to the open sky. Such a person is the realized soul and he is the man of real knowledge and wisdom. He has full control on his breath. He forgets death 21687 times per day; the number of times he breaths. By suspending his breath, he can be with death /spirit. He has full command to be with life or to be with death as per his wishes.

Desires come from the depth of the heart from Jeevatma; and are instruments to force an individual to live to fulfill them; he fulfills them through planning in his mind and by execution through his ego. Food is the cause of extension of life; and it causes breath to digest the food. Food gives energy to live but it is illusion to think that one lives by food only. One can live on water and gradually can switch on living entirely by the energy of the breath. Air, we breathe, has all the elements that can keep our body fit and healthy, since through air our physical system extracts Pranic energy that gives basic support to live. Jeeva needs more number of breaths to digest the solid food and thus it is more under the influence of Maya. By minimizing quantity of solid food, one can gradually conquer Maya; he can then live more with the spirit; and get closely associated with the death. Food creates more desires; increases ego; and layers of Maya/illusions go on increasing on the Jeevatma. After fulfillment of one desire, another desire is poured in and thus this unending cycle of desires is continued. Thus Samhar Biza, extension of desires continued without any restrain that increases the love/desire to live, but fear of death always scares an individual. However, when the desires are diminished, one can be in a state of silence. Indeed death is a state of Absolute silence.

By diminishing of all the desires, and by suspension of breaths as well as awareness, one can get the glimpses of enlightenment by the grace of Almighty; thus he can become immortal. Away from the food, breath and consciousness lead a Sadhaka to the doorsteps of death being in this life. Becoming pure Satvik, living on just water and finally on air/Prana, increases the soul light that helps to merge the soul in to the Supernal; and this gives the experience of death in life.

This discloses the mystery of death in life and life beyond death. Only Jeeva passes through the agony of death; soul is supreme and it beyond life and death. Realizing the soul light being in this life removes the curtain of death; and thus one becomes liberated from the pains of life and death forever. He becomes the enlightened soul and this must be the highest aim of one's life.

(D) 18.4 Simultaneous Existence of Life and Death in the Life

Every one of us is surprised to know that life and death exist simultaneously in the process of existence in our life. In every breath each one of is born and die. This process goes on life long. In the breathing cycle, as the fresh breath goes in, one gets life with vitality and as the breath goes out, he dies instantaneously till the next fresh breath is resumed. If the next fresh breath does not come, life of the Jeeva is under stake. The time spend without breath till the fresh breath is not in i.e. the time spend in the void, indicates the death of the Jeeva in such moments. So life and death exist simultaneously in the span of life in this world in each breath cycle.

It is surprising to know that in our spinal cord, two serpents are closely intermingled to each other. One of them is visible snake that is the divine light in the life and other one is invisible, which is the black snake of death. Both these serpents are coiled together and projected with separate hoods. Both are anti-poles to each other: one is life giver and other one is the life taker. Both are complimentary to each other but have distinct functions. Human survival depends on both of them and survival is at stake, and not feasible if one of them becomes functionless. Snake of death, the black snake, consumes the toxins of the body and keeps it healthy. It helps to excrete toxins by Apana Prana, Apana Vayu and helps the Udana Prana to function. Snake of divine light moves the human life. Thus both life and death forces i.e. white and black snakes are in unison and love with each another. Their love is through breath. One takes the fresh breath and other exhausts the used breath and thus the continuity of breath in and out is suitably maintained. If the used breath is not out of the system, the fresh breath cannot enter. So, it is evident that fresh life can only come when process of death is actively continued. It must be remembered that death only brings fresh life, and so if there is no death, then there is no life. Life and death are continuum, neither death can exist without life and nor life can exist without death. Life is manifested Brahma, and death is un-manifested Brahma. Both are the separate poles of the same existence. Any birth ends up and leads to death, it is the law of the nature so one must not be scared of death. When each one of us dies with every breath then life beyond death and life prior to death are no more mystery. It is continuous unending process and parts of existence in different states. These are well experienced by the Self-realized souls.

Both white and black snakes i.e. Kundalini/divine force and death exist in Kula Chakra. In the wakeful and dream states, their existence is felt. In Sushupati state both are in the state of Rati i.e. they are in unison. In Turiya, firstly the blackness/darkness, which is the indication of the presence of black snake, is visible; this is prior to the appearance of soul light i.e. the presence of kundalini; the white snake. Turiya is the state of temporary death; the state of the lack of function; where the light of Kundalini is firstly consumed by the black snake of death. After consuming positive divine energy of light, this black snake gets engaged in its own assigned activities of withdrawing toxins of the physical system; and then only Kundalini, the serpent of divine light ascends and merges the soul with the Supernal.

The state of Sushupati is the root/location of the union of death and life where death acts as a role of the husband, and life acts as a role of wife. Wife as a sign of divinity and glamour acts as a divine power, and is brought up for the Godly activities. A husband, as the black snake; the death; engages himself for the mundane worldly activities of preserving; maintaining; cleaning and conserving the human body/form. Out of love, husband, the serpent of death takes care of life; his wife; the divine Kundalini power; helps her to boom up. Otherwise life; the wife; cannot be glamorous and boom up if death, the husband; does not co-operate. This is the real mystery of life and death in the span of life and spiritual evolution of a Sadhaka/spiritual aspirant.

Food is essential for living and it is properly digested by the interaction of various Pranas, and finally the intestines absorb Anna-Rasa and thus life moves. Black snake takes energy from Anna-Rasa for survival just by touching/kissing the white divine snake; thus it executes body functions to keep the body fit in all respects by removing excrete and other dead stuff of the body by creating Apana Vayu; and thus it makes/cleaning the path for the Kundalini to ascend to fulfill its final goal. The same food can kill the white snake when breath seizes and Pranas become functionless and food remained undigested; this undigested food, thus, turns into poison in the body. The same food, which is the source of energy for both the snakes, finally turns into the cause of their death. So Anna-Rasa, when consumed by these snakes, hunger appears, and when undigested causes death as if it swallows the serpents of life. As the serpents lay eggs, eat part of their eggs and hatch part of them that become snakes. In the same way food is both cause of life as well as death; and this all revolves around time, space and causation. So, in the nutshell Anna/food is Brahma—the life giver, and it is a death by itself, as explained.

Death is a degenerative force that gives life after a lapse of time under appropriate conditions, so death and life move together. Life and death is lovable, inseparable couple, and without couple there is no force. In human system two Kundalini powers exist as a couple in unison, which help each other, one preserves the body and other assists in mergence of the soul with the supernal. Similarly, God and Yoga- Maya, Brahma and Maya, manifested and un-manifested forces, life and death exist in unison and cannot be separated. This is the Srishti and mystery of God and its creation. This is the duality of life and death.

In Sri Vidya, Shiva and Shakti exist for the creation. For dissolution, same Shakti/power turns into the force of Goddess Kali to nullify the creation. So Shakti acts in both ways as the mother of creation and mother of dissolution. Similarly, there is a same force, which gives life and causes the death. This is the duality of the creation and the mystery of the unknown. The most surprising factor is the fear of death in the human mind that makes a human being to love life very intimately and does not want to die and this is the Maya. The knowledge/realization of this duality of life and death is the basis of human's mind evolution; its churning enriches him with the secret of the unknown that both death and life are one and the same. One need not love one and hate /dislike other. Both are in continuum, one after the other. Both cannot be disintegrated, distracted, they are always in unison; however neither of one is permanent. Consciousness and awareness of human mind does not allow him to understand/apprehend this secret of the Almighty. This is the wonder of the Maya/illusion and even great yogis cannot penetrate in this secret of Maya as consciousness, and just revolve around it without taking the vertical path to transact its peripheral boundary.

Only penetration of the consciousness at the Dhahara Chakra can give the enlightenment of the secrets of life and death by the grace of Almighty. One can become the part of Almighty force by integrating and disintegrating his own body as per His will. Yoga can only teach the art of taking away the astral body that can enter to some other body i.e. Pragnya – body. However, the enlightenment from the source light can uplift the Sadhaka to such a high level where he can disintegrate his body in five elements and again integrate the body any where in the universe and thus can make astral travel by the God's grace.

Mount Smeru is the region of the saints where one can reach only through astral body. Symbala region of Tibet is famous for the saintly persons of the highest order. Mandela paintings are available there. Even stones are gems and diamonds in that region. No force on the earth by any means can reach there. It is only feasible by the astral travel; grace of Almighty; and blessings of Sri Sri Mahavtar Babaji.

(E) 18.5 Existence of Life in Death

Death is the end of present form/body but it is not the end of life. Death is a continuation of life in different dimension for some period of time before it takes some other form/body. After death, the life is all together different; it can be individual life being all-alone in different dimension; it can be combined life with others; or may be a cosmic life. However, it will be entirely different than the life in the present existence of name, form, environment, social interaction, capacity and the modes of living. The existence of life after death will be presently beyond known, but it will be continuum. Death is not the ultimate; it is like changing the cloths of the present life and change of environment for the Jeevatma. This is because the soul of the Jeeva is immortal and it is in cosmic oneness after the death, however, before death it is in the cage of the present form. Life continues in 84 lakhs species of the Jeevas therefore by any logical norm death is not the dead end of the existence. Soul can take any form as per the command of Almighty based on karmas, desires and attachments of the Jeeva. Life is basically transmigration after death from one form to another form as per the supreme commands.

Soul is the image of the whole. It is the reflection of the cosmic whole in the human being as the reflection of moon in the pot containing water. As and when the pot breaks, form/shape of the pot is destroyed; water spills but original moon remains as it is; however, its image from the pot disappears. In the same way, soul disappears after death from the human form since it is the part of the cosmic oneness; it merges with the supernal; but nothing happens beyond this. Death has no relevance to the eternal soul. Death is like breakage of the pot/body and five elements, from which the pot/body is made of, combine/dissolve gradually with those similar existing elements of the cosmos. On death only human body is crumpled but there is not the loss of elements of the body; it has; and also not any effect on the soul. As the pot is destroyed water in the pot is spilled and gets evaporated; this process may be compared to the human breath that disappears after it comes out from the body in the existing oneness of the universe and becomes the part of it. In this way present body/form is destroyed as the soul leaves and merges with supernal till the re-birth takes place in different form/body in the cosmic timeless time. This time variation can be a few years to a few hundred/thousand years. It is beyond the apprehension of the Jeeva and all this is governed by the mysterious means of the Absolute-Absolute.

The crumpled body/house/form cannot be repaired as the soul leaves so the Jeevatma has to get in new house/form as assigned by the Almighty to the Jeeva. After death, mind has no role to play since body, which the mind is looking after, is crumpled. So, immediately after the death, mind enters/combines the soul along with Jeeva. However, for a few microseconds before death, mind is liberated since it becomes functionless, and Jeeva enters in the stage of coma i.e. the stage of unawareness, before Jeeva is merged with the soul; thus Jeevatma (jeeva with soul) and mind leaves the body. Mind is a function of I-ness of the soul till the human body exists. Also, human life before death is governed and regulated by the mind under the supreme light of the soul resting in the Dhahara Chakra. That is the reason a few persons after death remember their own past lives. It is neither hallucination and nor imagination of any kind. It is the science of parapsychology that has proved the phenomenon of re-birth. There are number of living examples who know their past births/lives. That is the reason the past tendencies are reflected in most of the people from the early age itself. In the nutshell, mind of the Jeeva that was merged in the soul, immediately after the death, remembers the events of the past life; and is able to manifest the past tendencies without much affords.

The key points of existence of life in death may be summarized as:

Death is a mystery of life;

Life is inseparable from death;

Death is a continuation of life;

Life is a death and death is a life;

Death is the shifting of the focus from one form to another;

Death is a transmigration of life to another form.

(F) 18.6 Real Experience of Death

The number of cases has been reported from time to time in the Newspapers for those persons who have experienced death very closely and later returned to normal living. These are verifiable cases who remember their past lives, names in past lives and various incidences to have sufficient prove that life beyond death is a continuation even after physical death in the present life. Modern science has also proved it and presently there is basically no doubt on this proven and established thinking; what are we today has some close linkage with our past lives, although we do not remember all this.

The science of parapsychology has scientifically brought out the time of death in the past life and details of the past births. To establish these facts, the technique of hypnotic regression has been successfully implemented; in this technique the medium/concern person was taken layer by layer / step by step to the past lives and his narrations were recorded; documented; and scientifically analyzed. Later recording of all the statements, records and various old linkages were practically verified. Even the voice and language of the medium under hypnotic regression was found to be different, and matched to those times when he was alive. Thus the details of number of past births and how he faced death many times were brought up. These are the scientific facts beyond facts that confirm the life beyond death; and rebirth of Jeeva again and again confirming that life is a continuation even after multiple deaths. Also, this confirms beyond doubt that mind with its net experience with its condensed thinking merges with the soul at the time of death and discards the crumpled body.

In the forthcoming birth, the same mind with its past-condensed memories appears in different body/form; and undergoes actions/ reactions in the present life as deemed. The obligated net knowledge of the past life is preserved in the mind in a mysterious way at the time of death. By hypnotic regression, net experience of the past life has been brought out; however, in a conscious stage, the medium/the concerned person do not remember what all he spoke of the past life during hypnotic state. It is indeed mystery beyond mystery. This confirms scientifically that soul has the capacity to re-incarnate; the net knowledge of the past life remains and never lost. It is not the hallucination and nor the fobea/symbdrom. General Collar by his experiments on parapsychology has proved the rebirth theory of the Indian origin. This is not based on the Gene's of a person. This may be because of the certain type of chemicals absorption in the brain from the cosmic origin or from the inner system itself that remind him of the past lives under hypnotic regression or otherwise. However, what so ever may be the cause, but fact remains that it justifies the theory of re-birth, and life beyond death without an iota of doubt.

Furthermore, Dr.Rice in his book on, "Many Lights and Many Masters" has brought out many cases of re-births and proved/ justified the existence of life beyond death. He has vividly brought out that at the time of death: the body turns black; mind enters into the stage of coma instantaneously after the death; later soul, Jeeva and mind merge; experience of life is recorded in nutshell in a mysterious way; finally astral body with life long experience leaves the physically dead body. Then from a distance astral body witnesses the physically dead body and then passes through the big dark tunnel and finds light at the end of the tunnel. This light is a divine light; the light of the master spirit/Almighty; and based on His instructions the astral body may go back to the physically dead body and may revive it again. The revived body remembers this experience in some way or the other if the astral body is re-coupled to it. On the contrary, if master spirit/God does not desire, then astral body may not merge/return back to the dead body and then only actual death occurs.

Scientifically it has been proved that some force is released from body at the time of death and goes to Vasu Loka; Rudra Loka; or Aditya Loka. This is the migration of the soul; coupled with mind and Jeeva; from the dead body to take up another birth in due course after spending time in these Lokas. Very few souls get salvation based on their virtues. But most of the souls take re-birth in the world after experiencing Punaya/blessings or punishment after death in one of these Lokas. This all depends as per the wish of Almighty and His judgment based on His norms.

In the nutshell literature on parapsychology based on scientific research has left no doubt on the phenomenon of life beyond death; re-birth theory; and life continuum after life.

(G) 18.7 Mysterious Relation of Sandhya with Life/Death

In between the two breaths i.e. out going and the fresh breath that is on threshold to enter the human system, one remains without breathe for a fraction of a second. The interval without breath is the span of death. In this interval one is with the spirit/supernal unknowingly. If consciously one can understand and experience this mystery of the divine nature, one can unfold the secret of death.

Each one of us is the blossom of death about 21600 times per day; the number of times one breaths; however this duration is extremely small. But, if it is integrated considering that one breathes approximately 10 times a minute; taking 6 seconds for each breath with a gap/interval of one second between the two consecutive breaths; then it is not difficult to assess that a person remains nearly 30 minutes without breath per day. In other words 15-20 hrs per month; about 8-10 days per annum and in total life span of 80 years, about 800 days that is approximately 3% of the life span; he is without breath; and remains with the death/spirit/Supernal in totality.

By meditation; by Shunayaka technique; and by consciously observing the breath one can extend this period even up to 10%-15% and can experience death in this life; and can be with the Supernal by his efforts and with the grace of Almighty. Mind becomes very silent if consciously this time interval is increased without any stress. It can even become the continuum experience to be with the Absolute. This helps to draw direct cosmic energy from the Absolute as and when it is needed by his physical system; gradually his system will be filled with divine light and divine energy. This increases the life span; however, the spiritual aspirant may not have any desire to prolong the life; since for him life is death and death is life; both are same for him. He becomes Jeewan Mukta/liberated soul by the grace of Almighty just by increasing the time interval between two consecutive breaths. This is the basic mystery of mysteries and secret of life and death and as well life beyond death. Thus he is with the source light of the Absolute.

To be with the source light and Supernal is Sandhya. Sandhya is performed at the time of twilight i.e. when night is going to transform in to day light and when day is going to step in to night.

This transmigration/transit time interval is termed as Sandhya, and Pooja/worship is carried out during this interval. In terms of yoga it is the time interval between two consecutive breaths when used breath is on the way out from the body; and fresh breath is awaited to enter. This breathless state of microsecond is the natural Sandhya and worship/pooja interval. This is the span/time interval when life and death are closely knitted and one is with the Supernal. An advanced spiritual aspirant can do Sandhya with every breath and can be with the Absolute 21600 times a day. He can draw all the time more and more energy from the cosmos. Thus Sandhya becomes continuum with time. This may become even without awareness and Sadhaka experiences the blessings of Samadhi being with the divine light and enjoying the nectar of divinity. So Sandhya is not the ritual as being performed but it is the yogic mergence with the Supernal by worshipping and extending the interval between the consecutive breaths. This is from Sri Vidya, which is the mother of all the religions. This brings a spiritual aspirant to the stage of enlightenment that is the source knowledge and beyond this no knowledge is required. This gives light to the soul and oneness to time, space and causation. One becomes silent and experiences complete silence within him self, and gets the full glimpses of death being alive and is enlightened. In this transcendental state mind, intellect and consciousness disappear and merges with soul; and soul merges with the cosmic consciousness. This is the fundamental science of microcosm and others are only the applied sciences.

Enlightenment brings the knowledge of fundamental science i.e.: knowledge of secret of death; permanent/absolute silence; super consciousness; elongation of life span; migration to the better world after death; and so on.

Astral body after death, travel towards Vasu Loka, and then to Rudra Loka. In Vasu Loka astral body is given opportunity to shed vices, to improve, and if succeeded then it is allowed to go to Rudra Loka by the master spirit/Almighty. In this Loka if astral body becomes pure and totally desire-less, then as pure soul it is qualified to go to Aditya Loka. Here the soul is liberated from the cycles of birth and death and merges with the Supernal. Later, if required by

Almighty, this pure soul is sent as an Avatara/incarnation to Bhu Loka—in this world. Thus Jeevatma gets salvation by the austerities, and blessings of the omnipresent, omnipotent and omniscient energy source—the Almighty.

Furthermore, there are namely two Margas/ways for Self-realization namely Dhum Raj Marga and Achi Raja Marga/Aditya Marga. Dhum Raj Marga is the ritualistic path, the path of earning Puniya and Dharma etc. It is the path of Skama. Aditya Marga is the path of Nishkama. It is the path of worship of light without any Sankalpa/thoughts/desires. This is the supreme path, expressed by Yama to Nichiketa who disclosed him the secrets of death. This is the direct path of mergence with Supernal without any Sankalpa. In this path, the breath is to be suspended and gap between breaths needs to be extended; then only brain chemical is formed beyond the bio-spiritual atoms or from the cosmos energy brain cells are activated; and then only one recollects his past births and this discloses the mystery of death; life beyond death; and continuation of life after life.

(H) 18.8 Possibility of Birth as a Human Being After the Death

Life is a continuation after death; but, whether a person after death will take birth as a human being or not; cannot be predicted; it all depends on the judgment of the mysterious power of the Almighty after the death; it is based on his involvement in the divine activities during the span of his life. He may take birth in prosperous spiritual family in the forth coming birth or he may not be born again, will be decided by Almighty; it is based on his evolution and by the Will and grace of the God. He may become even Jeevan Mukta based on his deeds.

In case as a human being if he has not leaded discriminative life and did not cultivate desired virtues in his life span, he may take birth not as a human being. God by His discrimination may throw him back to 84 lakhs of birth cycles before he is again permitted to take birth as a human being. Human birth is considered as the last birth in the cosmic evolution. If he, after taking birth, as a human being, abuses his birth and spends his life in vices then it is not necessary that after death he again takes birth as a human being. If he is fully trapped in Maya during his life span then religious activities will not have any significance for him. Such a person does not follow the path of the soul for his evolution; penance of any kind does not have any significance for him; positive thinking and feeling do not attract him; and he is away from the path of Snatan Dharma. He is never involved in even in religious rituals; and spirituality is not even in his dream world; then there is remote chance that such a person is allowed by the Almighty to take birth as a human being.

Such human beings are recycled in the cycle of births and deaths till there occurs some degree of evolution in them before they are permitted to take birth as human beings.

Outwardly we all are mostly alike but inwardly each one of us is an entirely different and has unique personality. Close proximity only reveals the real basic nature and build up of the inner personality of an individual to another. Resonance occurs when two pure souls are in proximity. Divine throbbing is the resultant effect of this cause that brings precious offering of spiritual divine light to the society; mankind; that remains forever. The appearance of this book is the outcome of such an ever-lasting phenomenon that illuminates the kindle light in heart of souls desired for the Self-realization.

Seekers, who follow the divine path to know thyself, discharging worldly duties, have to face lot of intrinsic problems before they are evolved. Now a day, basically, no personal advance guidance of higher nature and direction are available, and thus number of their queries remains unresolved. This book has been written as an essential essence to give solutions to the various queries by scientific integration on inner human life in the form of questions/ answers.

This book has been brought out by inspiration and grace of the Cosmic Power; it is the outcome of being in divine path; and the solution of in-depth retrieval of subjective knowledge ascertained through silent communication. The book is the scientific integration of life force; divine light; supreme romance; mind; fate; mantra; yantra; tantra; type of breaths; various pranas and their origin ; happiness and stresses; illusion and its role; atma & jeevatma; astral body; importance of silence; death in life; mystery of life; and deals with the depth of many unknowns.

This unique book is the integration of subjective science of inner human life for the benefit of mankind; seekers of truth; for health and happiness; for transformation of personality; longevity of life, to take step into "Being"; to be beyond time & space with discontinuities for a human being to fulfill the primary purpose of life —— the Self– realization.